Cambridge Opera Handbooks

Alban Berg
Wozzeck

CAMBRIDGE OPERA HANDBOOKS

This is a series of studies of individual operas written for the opera-goer or record-collector as well as the student or scholar. Each volume has three main concerns: historical, analytical and interpretative. There is a detailed description of the genesis of each work, the collaboration between librettist and composer, and the first performance and subsequent stage history. A full synopsis considers the opera as a structure of musical and dramatic effects, and there is also a musical analysis of a section of the score. The analysis, like the history, shades naturally into interpretation: by a careful combination of new essays and excerpts from classic statements the editors of the handbooks show how critical writing about the opera, like the production and performance, can direct or distort appreciation of its structural elements. A final section of documents gives a select bibliography, a discography, and guides to other sources. Each book is published both in hard covers and as a paperback.

Published titles

Richard Wagner: *Parsifal* by Lucy Beckett
W. A. Mozart: *Don Giovanni* by Julian Rushton
C. W. von Gluck: *Orfeo* by Patricia Howard
Igor Stravinsky: *The Rake's Progress* by Paul Griffiths
Leoš Janáček: *Kát'a Kabanová* by John Tyrrell
Giuseppe Verdi: *Falstaff* by James A. Hepokoski
Benjamin Britten: *Peter Grimes* by Philip Brett
Giacomo Puccini: *Tosca* by Mosco Carner
Benjamin Britten: *The Turn of the Screw* by Patricia Howard
Richard Strauss: *Der Rosenkavalier* by Alan Jefferson
Claudio Monteverdi: *Orfeo* by John Whenham
Giacomo Puccini: *La bohème* by Arthur Groos and Roger Parker
Giuseppe Verdi: *Otello* by James A. Hepokoski
Benjamin Britten: *Death in Venice* by Donald Mitchell
W. A. Mozart: *Die Entführung aus dem Serail* by Thomas Bauman
W. A. Mozart: *Le nozze di Figaro* by Tim Carter
Hector Berlioz: *Les Troyens* by Ian Kemp
Claude Debussy: *Pelléas et Mélisande* by Roger Nichols and Richard Langham Smith

Alban Berg
Wozzeck

DOUGLAS JARMAN

Principal Lecturer, School of Academic Studies
Royal Northern College of Music

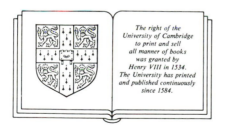

The right of the
University of Cambridge
to print and sell
all manner of books
was granted by
Henry VIII in 1534.
The University has printed
and published continuously
since 1584.

CAMBRIDGE UNIVERSITY PRESS

Cambridge
New York   New Rochelle   Melbourne   Sydney

Published by the Press Syndicate of the University of Cambridge
The Pitt Building, Trumpington Street, Cambridge CB2 1RP
32 East 57th Street, New York, NY 10022, USA
10 Stamford Road, Oakleigh, Melbourne 3166, Australia

First published 1989

Printed in Great Britain at the University Press, Cambridge

British Library cataloguing in publication data
Jarman, Douglas
Alban Berg, Wozzeck. – (Cambridge opera
handbooks).
1. Opera in German. Berg, Alban. Wozzeck –
Critical studies
I. Title
782.1′092′4

Library of Congress cataloguing in publication data
Jarman, Douglas.
Alban Berg, Wozzeck / Douglas Jarman.
    p.   cm. – (Cambridge opera handbooks)
Bibliography. |
Discography.
Includes index.
ISBN 0 521 24151 0 ISBN 0 521 28481 3 (pbk)
1. Berg, Alban, 1885–1935. Wozzeck. I. Title. II. Title:
Wozzeck. III. Series.
ML410.B47J3 1989
782.1′092′4 – dc19   88-15965   CIP

ISBN 0 521 24151 0 hard covers
ISBN 0 521 28481 3 paperback

ME

Contents

List of illustrations   *page*   vii
Acknowledgments   ix

1   Introduction   1
2   The play and the libretto   7
3   Musical background and composition   16
4   Synopsis   25
5   The formal design   41
6   Act III scene 4: an analysis   52
7   A suggested interpretation   59
8   Stage history: the premiere and subsequent   69
    performances

Documents   110

1   Karl Emil Franzos   Georg Büchner (1901)   111
2   Hugo Beiber   Wozzeck and Woyzeck (1914)   129
3   Erwin Stein   Alban Berg and Anton von   132
                     Webern (1922)
4   Fritz Heinrich Klein   Alban Berg's 'Wozzeck' (1923)   135
5   Ernst Viebig   Alban Berg's 'Wozzeck':   139
                     a contribution to the problem of
                     opera (1923)
6   Emil Petschnig   Creating atonal opera (1924)   143
7   Alban Berg   The musical forms in my opera   149
                     'Wozzeck' (1924)
8   Alban Berg   A word about 'Wozzeck' (1927)   152
9   Alban Berg   A lecture on 'Wozzeck' (1929)   154

vi   *Contents*

Notes   171
Bibliography   175
Discography   177
Index   178

Plates

1 *Piano Sonata No. 4 in D minor*   *page* 91
   One of five piano sonatas which Berg began while
   studying with Schoenberg. The opening bars of
   the abandoned fourth sonata became the opening
   bars of the final orchestral interlude of *Wozzeck*.
   (Music Department, Austrian National Library,
   MS F 21/Berg 48)
2 *Berlin, December 1925*   92
   Sketch by Panos Aravantinos for the set of Act I
   scene 4 (Universal Edition)
3 *Oldenburg, March 1929*   93
   Act II scene 1 with Josef Lex (Wozzeck) and
   Emma Friedrichs (Marie). Set by Ernst Rufer
4 *Aachen, February 1930*   94
   Berg with members of the cast and the production
   staff. Heinrich Strohm (director), Helmut Jürgens
   (designer), Berg, Richard Bitterauf (Wozzeck),
   Alice Bruhn (Marie), Paul Pella (conductor)
5 *Aachen, February 1930*   95
   Act II scene 3. Richard Bitterauf (Wozzeck),
   Alice Bruhn (Marie)
6 *Aachen, February 1930*   96
   Act II scene 5. Richard Bitterauf (Wozzeck),
   Anton Ludwig (Drum Major)
7 *Aachen, February 1930*   97
   Act III scene 2. Richard Bitterauf (Wozzeck),
   Alice Bruhn (Marie)
8 *Darmstadt, February 1931*   98
   Lothar Schenk von Trapp (designer). Act I scene 2.
   Albert Lohman (Wozzeck), Johannes Schocke
   (Andres)

vii

9 *Darmstadt, February 1931*   99
  Act II scene 1. Anita Mittrovic (Marie)
10 *Darmstadt, February 1931*   100
  Act II scene 4
11 *Darmstadt, February 1931*   101
  Act II scene 5. Albert Lohman (Wozzeck), Joachim
  Sattler (Drum Major)
12 *Philadelphia, March 1931*   102
  Sketch by Robert Edmund Jones for Act I scene 4
  (Universal Edition)
13 *Frankfurt, April 1931*   103
  Ludwig Sievert (designer). Act III scene 2. Jan Stern
  (Wozzeck), Erna Recka (Marie) (Universal Edition)
14 *Wuppertal, May 1931*   104
  Harry Breuer (designer). Act I scene 1. Johannes Drath
  (Wozzeck), Peter Markwort (Captain)
15 *Wuppertal, May 1931*   105
  Act II scene 2. Johannes Drath (Wozzeck), Peter
  Markwort (Captain), Walter Hagner (Doctor)
16 *Leipzig, October 1931*   106
  Walter Brugmann (designer). Act I scene 1. Karl August
  Neumann (Wozzeck), Reiner Minten (Captain)
17 *Leipzig, October 1931*   107
  Act II scene 2. Karl August Neumann (Wozzeck),
  Reiner Minten (Captain), Ernst Osterkamp (Doctor)
18 *Leipzig, October 1931*   108
  Act II scene 5. Karl August Neumann (Wozzeck),
  August Seider (Drum Major)
19 *Zurich, October 1931*   109
  Sketch by Karl Groening-Altona for the set of
  Act III scene 2

Acknowledgments

The present book began life as a collaboration between myself and the distinguished American composer and Berg scholar George Perle. Although the pressure of Professor Perle's other commitments eventually forced him to withdraw from the venture, I would like to take this opportunity to thank him for the help which he gave while the book was being written and for his unfailingly useful and stimulating comments on the earlier drafts. Anyone familiar with Professor Perle's writings on *Wozzeck*, and especially with the first of his two volumes on the *Operas of Alban Berg*, will realise the extent to which I am indebted to his work.

I am grateful to the Director, Hofrat Dr Gunter Brosche, and to Rat Dr Rosemary Moravec of the Musiksammlung of the Austrian National Library in Vienna; to Universal Edition (Alfred A. Kalmus Ltd) and to Universal Edition, Vienna and to its archivist Dr Elisabeth Knessl; to the Directors of the Alban Berg Stiftung and to Mr Antony Hodges, Librarian of the Royal Northern College of Music, Manchester.

My especial thanks are due to Regina Busch for her help in locating many of the photographs reproduced in this book and for her generosity and kindness throughout the final stages of preparation.

1 *Introduction*

On 5 May 1914, a young man called Paul Elbogen attended the first Viennese performance of Georg Büchner's *Woyzeck*[1] at the Residenzbühne on Rotenturmstrasse. Sixty-seven years later Elbogen recalled the occasion in the following words:

We young people knew the play very well from Franzos's publication. A German actor, Albert Steinrück, rude and rather brutal, played Wozzeck. I sat in the gallery of the little Kammerspiele. Four rows behind me sat Alban Berg, whom I greeted as I came in because I had known him very well for years. They played the drama for three hours without the smallest interruption in complete darkness. Indescribably excited and enthusiastic I stood up amidst wild applause, met Alban Berg a few steps behind me. He was deathly pale and perspiring profusely. 'What do you say?' he gasped, beside himself. 'Isn't it fantastic, incredible?' Then, already taking his leave, 'Someone must set it to music.'[2]

It is not often that we are lucky enough to have such a description of what seems to have been the precise moment at which a composer decides to write an opera. What Elbogen witnessed was the origin of a work that occupies a unique place in the history of opera and the history of twentieth-century music.

The economics of opera production are such that the repertoire of most opera houses tends to be conservative, based, for the most part, on a number of accepted classics from the eighteenth and nineteenth centuries which it is known will attract a large audience. The few twentieth-century operas that have become established as part of this repertoire are usually those that employ a relatively traditional musical language. The two operas of Alban Berg are exceptional in that both have entered the repertoire and both use a musical language that was, and to many people still is, radical. *Wozzeck* was the first, and remains the only atonal opera to be regularly performed and generally accepted as a classic of twentieth-century music theatre; *Lulu* (although labouring, until recently, under the disad-

1

vantage of having to be performed as an incomplete two-act torso) is the only twelve-note opera to be performed as part of the standard repertoire.

Both *Wozzeck* and *Lulu* are exceptional in other respects as well. From the earliest beginnings of the form, in the last years of the sixteenth century, the problem of opera has been that of reconciling, or even simply balancing, the demands of the music with those of the dramatic action. Whatever the stylistic features of the musical language employed, musical structures have their own, purely musical, logic, their own tensions and relaxations, their own inherent need for repetition, variation, unity and diversity. The extent to which these musical needs have been regarded as taking precedence over, or as being subordinate to, the possibly conflicting demands of the drama has varied from period to period and from composer to composer. But some kind of reassessment of the relationship between the demands of the music and those of the dramatic action has been the basis of every attempt at operatic reform from those of Monteverdi and Gluck to those of Wagner, of Busoni, and of Weill.

In the formal design of *Wozzeck* Berg offered an ingenious and highly original solution to this perennial problem. If Berg's solution has not become the model for later composers it is perhaps because his handling of the relationship between musical form and dramatic action in *Wozzeck* represents an achievement of such stature and of so peculiarly individual and personal a nature that there were few ways in which it could be developed by his successors. In the event, only Berg himself was able, in *Lulu*, to develop further the formal ideas upon which the musico-dramatic structure of *Wozzeck* was based.

Wozzeck also represents a radical extension of the range of the operatic repertoire in that it deals with subjects and with mental and emotional states that had not, until that time, been regarded as suitable for operatic treatment. There had, of course, been earlier operas in which characters had gradually been driven insane, and, indeed, the 'mad scene' and the musical and dramatic conventions for handling such scenes had become something of an operatic tradition by the end of the nineteenth century. But no opera before *Wozzeck* had had a psychotic anti-hero as its central character, and no opera before *Wozzeck* (and, perhaps, none since) had depicted mental instability in such a way that the audience shared this instability, rather than simply observing its outward effects.

The expressionist language of the first decades of the twentieth century was peculiarly well suited to deal with such extreme mental and emotional states. Expressionism, an artistic movement in which reality or aspects of reality were deliberately distorted in order to express the artist's emotional response to a subject, dominated all the arts in Germany and Austria from about 1910 to the early 1920s. The movement had its origins in the last decades of the nineteenth century, in the work of painters such as Van Gogh, who, in the 1880s, described how he consciously exaggerated colours and forms in his paintings so as to express his feelings about, rather than simply record, what he saw. By the mid 1890s and the early 1900s many artists (such as Edvard Munch, Emil Nolde, Matisse and the *Fauves* in France, and the *Die Brücke* group of painters in Dresden) were painting works in which the shapes and colours of the natural world were subjected to violent distortions for expressive purposes.

Although written some seventy-five years before German expressionism became an established movement, Büchner's *Woyzeck* had in it many elements which the expressionists regarded as anticipations of their own interests and concerns. Thus, in the Büchner play as in the works of the expressionists themselves, reality seemed (as Wilhelm Worringer wrote in 1912 in one of the key documents in the development of German expressionism) to be 'transformed into a spectrally heightened and distorted actuality. Everything becomes weird and fantastic. Behind the visible appearance of things lurks its caricature. . .and so all actual things become grotesque.'[3] Similarly the ominous and uncaring world that Büchner's Woyzeck inhabits seemed to mirror what Herbert Read has called 'the unease and terror which man may feel in the presence of a nature fundamentally hostile and inhuman', to express what they themselves sought to express in their work through the 'emotive distortions of natural forms'.[4]

Berg's opera presents us with such a 'heightened and distorted' actuality rather than with a documentary realism. There is no attempt in *Wozzeck*, as there is in Britten's *Peter Grimes* for example, to depict the title figure as a misfit in an otherwise 'normal' society in which people are going about their everyday business and leading their recognizably ordinary lives. The picture with which Berg presents us is that of a society in which the underprivileged are at the mercy of an unfeeling, selfish and sadistic ruling class, a class that keeps the less fortunate in their place through its financial domination and its appeals to vacuous moral ideals. It is a society that is so inhuman and so grotesque that the simple but good Wozzeck is inevitably driven to his crime by his poverty, his suffering and his very simplicity. Only in the final orchestral interlude, when Wozzeck is dead and the action of the opera is ended – and even then, only when the curtain is down and the music removed from the characters and events on stage – does the composer's own sympathy for his chief character introduce an element of humanity into the work.

As some of the reviews quoted in Chapter 8 show, many of the critics, and particularly the English critics writing in the 1950s, dismissed the opera as being little more than the hysterical and depressing case history of a psychotic mind. It is true that much of the extraordinary dramatic impact of Berg's opera springs from the fact that, at crucial moments, we in the audience are forced to experience what Wozzeck experiences and to feel the strength of his hallucinatory vision of the world. But what we see in *Wozzeck* is not simply the projection of a deranged mind. Nor is it only the picture of a deranged, unfeeling society. It is, as we shall see, a protest against both the social order and, as the musical structure makes clear, the nature of the world itself; an expression of what, in the passage quoted above, Herbert Read called the 'terror which man may feel in the presence of a nature that is fundamentally hostile and inhuman'.

In Berg's hands the language of musical expressionism – of a music that constantly exploits the expressive tension at the borderline between tonality and atonality – becomes a marvellously appropriate means of representing Wozzeck's mental condition. Before the end of the first decade of the twentieth century the musical language would have been unable to express the instability of a character such as Wozzeck with the force that we feel in Berg's opera. On the other hand, it is doubtful whether after 1925, when the composers of the Second Viennese School were developing a more formal and systematic approach to the creation of a new musical grammar, even Berg himself would have been interested in depicting Wozzeck's condition in the kind of musical language that he had used so effectively a few years earlier. When, in 1928, Berg saw a revival of the Berlin production of *Wozzeck* he observed that the orchestra sounded beautiful 'even with my present taste which has rather moved away from that style of composition'.[5] It was one of the fortunate chances of artistic history that the right, but long ignored, play should find the right composer at the right stage of both his own development and the development of the musical language.

Apart from the various student works that have come to light since the death of Helene Berg, the composer's widow, in 1976 (works which are, in the main, so stylistically immature that they can be dismissed as being little more than run-of-the-mill apprentice efforts), it is a striking feature of Berg's output that there are no false starts, no abandoned, half-completed, works, no series of preparatory pieces leading up to each of the mature masterpieces. There are no orchestral songs before the extraordinary achievement of the *Altenberg Lieder*, no orchestral works in preparation for the Three Orchestral Pieces, Op. 6, no early chamber works pointing in the direction of the String Quartet, no solo concertos preceding the Violin Concerto. Most astonishing of all is the fact that there are no stage works leading up to *Wozzeck*; that, with no theatrical or operatic experience other than that acquired by seeing performances of the works of others, Berg should immediately demonstrate so masterly a grasp of musical timing and dramatic effectiveness and that he should do so in a work of such extraordinary orginality and individuality as his first opera.

The first part of this book is concerned with the literary and musical background of the opera: Chapter 2 with the origins and history of Büchner's play and with the relationship between the play and the libretto, Chapter 3 with the development of Berg's own musical language before *Wozzeck* and with the composition of the opera. The second part deals with the work itself – the plot and the overall musical design in Chapters 4 and 5, the musico-dramatic structure of a single scene (Act III scene 4) in Chapter 6 and in Chapter 7 with a possible interpretation of the opera suggested by certain features of the musical design. Chapter 8 traces the stage history of the work from its premiere in 1925 onwards.

Unlike most of the other books in this series the present book contains no discussion of the collaboration between composer and librettist, since in order to realize his highly individual ideas about the way in which the musical and dramatic structures were to relate to one another Berg had to act as his own librettist.

The final section of the book presents a number of important historical documents and critical articles. The first two of these – Karl Emil Franzos's own report of his discovery and first publication of the work and Hugo Beiber on his discovery of the historical source – are concerned with the Büchner play. The remaining documents are concerned with the opera – Erwin Stein's 1922 essay on Berg and Webern (one of the first articles to draw attention to Schoenberg's two pupils); an article from a 1923 edition of *Musikblätter des Anbruch* by Berg's pupil Fritz Heinrich Klein, who prepared the vocal score of the opera; Ernst Viebig's essay (also dating from 1923) on Berg's privately printed score; the polemical exchange between Petschnig and Berg and, finally, Berg's own 'A word about "Wozzeck"' and his 1929 lecture on the opera.

The illustrations in the book (on pp. 91–109) should also be regarded as part of this documentary section since, with a single exception, they consist of photographs of productions, or of the sets for productions, staged during Berg's own lifetime.

2 The play and the libretto

Georg Büchner was born in Goddelau near Darmstadt on 17 October 1813. His father was the district physician and there had been doctors in the family from the sixteenth century onwards. Büchner himself studied medicine at the Universities of Strasbourg and Giessen from 1831 to 1834. In the autumn of 1836 he took up a post as lecturer in natural history at the University of Zurich. Three months later, on 19 February 1837, the twenty-three-year-old Büchner died of typhus.

Whilst a student at Strasbourg Büchner had become interested in and sympathetic towards the radical political ideas sweeping through Europe in the wake of the French Revolution of 1830. During his year of study at Giessen these sympathies led to his active involvement with an underground political group led by a Pastor Friedrich Ludwig Weidig. It was for Weidig's illegal political press that Büchners wrote his first work, *Der hessische Landbot* (*The Hessian Courier*), a protest against the economic plight of the local peasants and a denunciation of their exploiters, the rich landowners. The pamphlet was printed, in a much modified form, in July 1834, but was never distributed to the peasants for whom it was intended. The conspiracy was betrayed and two of Büchner's friends were arrested while smuggling copies of the pamphlet into Giessen. The authorities searched Büchner's own rooms, but since there was nothing that identified him as the author of the pamphlet or implicated him in the conspiracy, he remained free long enough to escape to his family in Darmstadt. Here he remained for several months, and then, knowing that his arrest was imminent, crossed the border into France and returned to Strasbourg.

With the exception of *Der hessische Landbot* the whole of Büchner's literary output was written during the last two years of his life – his first play, *Dantons Tod* (*Danton's Death*), in Darmstadt in the first two months of 1835, the prose narrative *Lenz* and the comedy

7

Leonce und Lena in Strasbourg in 1835–36, and *Woyzeck* in the final year of his life. Another play, *Pietro Aretino*, is supposed to have been completed but has disappeared; like Büchner's letters and diaries, the play may have been burned by his fiancée Minna Jaegle after his death.

Büchner based *Woyzeck* on a real event which had taken place in Leipzig some fifteen years earlier. In 1821 Johann Christian Woyzeck, an ex-soldier and barber, had murdered his mistress, a Frau Woost, for being unfaithful to him. At the subsequent trial the defence entered a plea of insanity on the ground that Woyzeck heard voices and was subject to hallucinations. However, the expert witness appointed as medical assessor by the court, Hofrat Dr J. C. A. Clarus, gave evidence that the accused could not be regarded as mentally unstable. The defence plea was turned down and Johann Christian Woyzeck was publicly executed in the market square in Leipzig on 27 August 1824. The case had aroused considerable interest and controversy, however, and in 1825 Clarus published an account of his examination of Woyzeck in the *Zeitschrift für Staatsarzneikunde*, a medical journal to which Büchner's father subscribed and occasionally contributed. Much of Büchner's play is based on the words of Woyzeck himself as they appear in Clarus's published report.

After Büchner's death the manuscript of *Woyzeck* lay ignored amongst his papers for almost forty years until the novelist Karl Emil Franzos undertook the preparation of a complete edition of Büchner's work in the mid 1870's. The task facing Franzos in preparing a first edition of *Woyzeck* was enormous. In the years between Büchner's death and Franzos's study of the *Woyzeck* manuscript the ink in which it was written had faded to such an extent that the text of the play had almost disappeared and could only be read after the pages had been treated with chemicals. Even after such treatment Büchner's 'microscopically small' handwriting was almost illegible. Indeed, Franzos had such difficulty in deciphering the manuscript that he even misread the name of the main character so that the play was originally published under the title *Wozzeck* (hence the title of Berg's opera) rather than under its correct title of *Woyzeck*. Franzos was also faced with other difficulties, for it quickly became apparent that there were different drafts of many of the scenes and that the ordering of the scenes in the manuscript gave no indication of the order in which the scenes were to appear in the final play. Working from the confused and hardly legible manuscript, Franzos established, as best he could, a text and a dramatically feasible ordering of the scenes and published the first edition of the play in 1879. In 1909, thirty years after the publication of the original edition, the ordering of the scenes was revised by Paul Landau in a new edition which otherwise left the Franzos text untouched. It was on this 1909 edition that Berg based his libretto.

Of Büchner's plays only *Dantons Tod* was published (in a distorted and mutilated version) during his lifetime and none was performed. *Leonce und Lena* was first staged by an amateur company in Munich in 1895, and *Dantons Tod*, likewise by an amateur company, in Berlin in 1902. The latter received its first professional production under Leopold Jessner in Hamburg in 1910 and then at the Deutsches Theater in Berlin in 1916 in a production by Max Reinhardt. *Woyzeck* was first produced in 1913 at the Residenztheater in Munich. By this time, however, Franzos's 1879 edition was well-known in avant-garde literary circles, for the play had been acclaimed by both the expressionist and the naturalist writers as a forerunner of their own work. Receiving its premiere on the eve of World War I, seventy-six years after the author's death, it seemed, in retrospect, to reflect the experience of the common soldiers who had suffered in that war; to the expressionists it was a play that reflected their own interest in exploring extreme mental and emotional states; to the new generation of artists who came to the fore after the war it seemed both to anticipate the revolutionary theatrical techniques of the period and, in its political and social stance, to embody the views held by many people in the immediate post-war years.

The end of the first war left the German people bewildered. The victory, which only a few months earlier had seemed assured, had crumbled by the autumn of 1918, and the ensuing peace brought only defeat and humiliation. Everything that they had suffered during the war – the deprivations, the sacrifice of nearly two million lives, the wounding of another four million soldiers – suddenly seemed to have been without point. They felt a sense of betrayal and resentment towards those who had led them into the war. It was a resentment that was eventually to find expression in the revolution which, beginning with the sailors' mutiny at Kiel and other North Sea ports in October 1918, led within less than a month to the abdication of the Kaiser and the founding of the Weimar Republic. But the sense of disillusionment encompassed not only the politicians and the military leaders responsible for the war and the subsequent defeat but extended to everything, including the arts, that seemed to represent the old order. Following the war many artists felt that the old art forms had been shown to be irrelevant and self-indulgent. Although Expressionism was still a major force in the arts of the Weimar Republic (the most famous of the German expressionist films, Robert Wiene's *The Cabinet of Dr Caligari*, for example, was made in 1919), many artists regarded it as 'a flight from the hard-edgedness of things'[1] consisting of nothing but 'symbolic vagaries and an intentionally indiscriminate jumble of colours, lines, distortions, words and concepts'.[2] To those artists who subscribed to these beliefs the new art should be objective, unemotional and have a direct social relevance: it should be a less élitist art than that of the pre-war years, an art that would speak directly to the ordinary man and that would be able to play a role in building the more just society which, it was hoped, would be the outcome of the new republic.

In music the 'new objectivity' (*Neue Sachlichkeit*) took many forms; the attempt to establish a new anti-Wagnerian opera in the works of Weill and Brecht, neoclassicism, Gebrauchsmusik, the interest in jazz, the deliberate cultivation of a simpler and more immediately comprehensible musical language in the work of Weill were all manifestations of the anti-elitist, anti-romantic attitude which characterized much of the music of the inter-war years.

To those who believed that the arts had a radical social role to play Büchner's drama, with its strong social message and its simple, down-to-earth language, was a model of what the new art should be and of how art might change society.

The attempt to cultivate a simpler, more popular style was not one with which the members of the Second Viennese School, and particularly Schoenberg and Webern, sympathized. 'It is self-evident', wrote Schoenberg a few months after the enormously successful Berlin premiere of *Die Dreigroschenoper* (*The Threepenny Opera*), 'that art which treats deeper ideas cannot address itself to the many. "Art for everyone": anyone regarding that as possible is unaware how "everyone" is constituted and how art is constituted.'[3] To Schoenberg, Weill's music was 'the only music in the world' in which he could find 'no quality',[4] while Dallapiccola has reported how Webern exploded into anger at the mere mention of Weill's name – 'What do you find of our great central European tradition in such a composer?'[5]

Although Berg shared Schoenberg's aesthetic position (and, if we are to believe Adorno's account of Berg's reaction to the successful premiere of *Wozzeck*, actually distrusted popular acclaim[6]), he was less bitterly opposed to Weill and the artistic movement that Weill represented than were his two colleagues. We know that Berg was interested enough in the so-called 'new opera' of Brecht to attend the rehearsals for *Der Aufstieg und Fall der Stadt Mahagonny* (*The Rise and Fall of the City of Mahagonny*) when it received a studio production in Vienna in 1932 under the baton of Berg's own pupil Gottfried Kassowitz.

Although Berg shared neither the aesthetic stance nor the overt political motivation of many of the young German artists of the time (and, indeed, Berg himself seems to have been relatively apolitical in the sense that he was neither a member of one of the numerous politically orientated artistic groups that sprang up at the time, nor was he actively involved in politics in the way that many of his friends and acquaintances were), he nonetheless had certain social attitudes in common with these artists and there can be little doubt that he saw in Büchner's play a humanitarian socialism which coincided with his own social and political attitudes.

In turning the play into an opera libretto Berg omitted a number of scenes which appear in the original. Seven scenes of the play he omitted entirely: scenes 5 and 6 of the Landau version (in which Wozzeck and Marie visit a fairground and watch a performance by a trained donkey); scene 8 (in which the Doctor lectures a group of students); scene 12 (between Wozzeck and Andres); scene 18 (in which Wozzeck buys the knife with which he will eventually murder Marie); Scene 20 (in which Wozzeck gives his coat to Andres); and the last scene, in the dissecting room after the murder, of which Büchner completed only the opening lines. Scene 14 (in which Wozzeck, alone, imagines that he hears the music of the dance band) and scene 19 (in which an old woman tells the children a fairy story) are also omitted, but elements of each of these scenes are grafted on to other scenes in the opera – the hearing of the dance music on to the barracks scene (Act II scene 5) and the telling of the fairy story on to Marie's speech in scene 17 of the Landau edition which becomes the first scene of Act III in the opera. Scenes 15 and 16 of the Landau edition were run together to form the barracks scene in the opera. The chart on pp. 12–15 shows the sequence of scenes in the play and the opera. Apart from omitting or reorganizing these scenes, Berg made no major changes to the play other than arranging the remaining scenes into three separate acts. Such changes as he did make seem to have been made during, and as a result of, work on the composition. Even the decision to organize the whole into three acts of five scenes each – a decision which one would have thought basic to the whole formal structure of the opera – seems to have been made at a relatively late stage of work on the composition.

With the exceptions mentioned above, the libretto of *Wozzeck* differs from Büchner's play only in the addition of production details that appear in neither the original manuscript nor in the Franzos–Landau edition, and in the various small textual modifications which Berg made in order to point the dramatic and musical relationships between different scenes or to underline the dramatic irony. In the first scene of the opera, for example, Berg rearranges Büchner's text so that the Captain's final sentence ends with the word 'langsam' ('slowly'). Since 'langsam' is the first word heard in the opera the scene thus ends with the same word with which it began, a relationship emphasized musically by the fact that the word is set to the same notes on both appearances. Berg's modification has the effect of drawing attention to the Captain's obsession with the subject of time and establishes the word 'langsam' as an important verbal leitmotive. In retrospect the 'langsam' of the opening scene acquires a bitterly ironic significance thanks to a stage direction which Berg adds to the penultimate scene of the opera. In Büchner the two passers-by who witness Wozzeck's death are anonymous. By specifying that the two passers-by should be the Captain and the Doctor, Berg not only underlines the criminal responsibility of the society of which these two characters are the most direct representatives, but is also able to ensure that the Captain's last word in the opera is 'schnell' ('quickly') – 'Doctor, Come quickly,' says the Captain as he hurries away from the scene of the tragedy. It is the only time in the opera when the Captain abandons his usual request that everyone do things 'nice and slowly.'

A number of small textual differences between the libretto of Act I scene 4, and the equivalent scene in the play seem to have been made for purely personal reasons. These will be discussed in Chapter 7.

Woyzeck: Büchner (Franzos/Landau)	*Wozzeck*: Berg
	ACT I
Scene 1 *A room*	*Scene 1* *The Captain's room.* *Early morning*
Woyzeck shaves the Captain.	

Scene 2 *Open country. The town in the* *distance* Woyzeck and Andres cut sticks.	*Scene 2* *Open country. The town in the* *distance. Late afternoon*
Scene 3 *The town* Marie watches the military band pass. She sings to the child. Woyzeck visits.	*Scene 3* *Marie's room. Evening*
Scene 4 *The Doctor's study* The Doctor examines Woyzeck.	*Scene 4* *The Doctor's study. A sunny* *afternoon*
Scene 5 *An open place. Booths* Marie and Woyzeck visit the fair.	—
Scene 6 *Inside one of the booths* Marie and Woyzeck watch a trained donkey perform.	—
Scene 7 *Street* The Drum Major seduces Marie.	*Scene 5* *Street before Marie's house* *door. Evening twilight*
Scene 8 *Courtyard at the Doctor's* The Doctor lectures to a group of students.	—

ACT II

Scene 9 *Room* Marie admires the earrings. Woyzeck discovers her.	*Scene 1* *Marie's room. Sunny morning*

Scene 10
Street
The Doctor and the Captain
meet Woyzeck and taunt him.

Scene 2
A street in the town. Day

Scene 11
Marie's room

Woyzeck confronts Marie.

Scene 3
Street before Marie's house.
Overcast day

Scene 12
Guard room
Woyzeck and Andres

—

Scene 13
Tavern
Woyzeck watches Marie dance
with the Drum major. He is
approached by the idiot.

Scene 4
Tavern garden. Late evening

Scene 14
Open Country. Night
Woyzeck hears voices and
music.

Scene 15
Barracks. Night

Unable to sleep, Woyzeck wakes
Andres.

Scene 5
Dormitory in the barracks.
Night

Scene 16
The yard of the barracks
The Drum Major taunts and
fights Woyzeck.

ACT III

Scene 17
Marie's room

Marie reads the Bible.

Scene 1
Marie's room. Night.
Candlelight

Scene 18
Pawn-shop
Woyzeck buys the knife.

—

Scene 19
Street. A sunny afternoon
Marie watches the children
playing. An old woman tells a   [The fairy story is incorporated
fairy story.   into Act III scene 1 above.]

Scene 20
Barracks
Woyzeck gives his coat to   —
Andres.

Scene 21   *Scene 2*
A path in the woods by a pond.   *A path in the woods by a pond.*
It is twilight   *Dusk*
Woyzeck murders Marie.

Scene 22   *Scene 3*
A pub   *A pub. Night. Dimly lit*
Woyzeck tries to get drunk.

Scene 23   *Scene 4*
A path in the woods by the   *The path in the woods by the*
pond. Night   *pond. Moonlit night as before*
Woyzeck drowns.

Scene 24   *Scene 5*
Early morning. In front of   *In front of Marie's house door.*
Marie's house   *Bright morning. Sunshine*
The children play.

Scene 25
Dissecting room
A doctor and a judge comment   —
on the murder.

3 *Musical background and composition*

If Büchner's *Woyzeck* was discovered and first performed at the 'right time', in the sense that the artistic and social thought of the 1910s and 1920s made the techniques and concerns of the play seem strikingly contemporary, it was also performed at a time when Berg's own musical language had developed to a stage at which it was peculiarly well suited to handle the extreme emotional and mental states depicted in the play.

Before Berg began to study with Schoenberg in 1904, his output consisted entirely of songs. There exist from this early period some fifty songs, most of which, while bearing witness to the young Berg's already highly developed literary tastes, reveal a musical ability that seems to be little more than average. Nothing demonstrates so clearly the profound influence that Schoenberg's teaching and Schoenberg's own music had upon the young student than does the contrast between the language and technical ability shown in these very early songs and those of Berg's first published composition.

The six years during which Berg studied with Schoenberg were vital years in Schoenberg's own development as a composer. The First String Quartet in D minor, on which Schoenberg was working when Berg first became his pupil, still speaks a harmonic language that is not far removed from the post-Wagnerian *Verklärte Nacht* (*Transfigured Night*) of five years earlier, vastly superior as it is in technical craftsmanship. Within the next five years Schoenberg had moved from the highly chromatic but nonetheless tonally-based language of his early works to the free atonality of the Five Orchestral Pieces, Op. 16, and *Erwartung*, works in which tonality, triadic harmony, and the very concept of consonance and dissonance have disappeared.

In the music of the classical composers the largest and smallest elements of the musical structure are all referable to a single organizational system. The relationships of chords to the tonic triad

16

and of keys to the tonic key, the tonal structure of an individual phrase, of a section, a movement, and of a complete work are all reflections, at different structural levels, of the same hierarchical system of relationships. Every aspect of tonal music, including the rhythmic and metric structure, is ultimately referable to the tonal hierarchy. In the *Harmonielehre*, his great textbook on traditional harmonic practice, Schoenberg describes the functions of tonality as being to unify and to articulate. By the late nineteenth century the complexity of the harmonic language and the increasingly free use of "foreign" chromatic notes had undermined the identity of the tonic key to such an extent that the large-scale, architectural function of tonality had become highly problematical. Remote keys were brought into close juxtaposition with the tonic and given the same emphasis as keys closely related to the tonic, the resolution of a dissonance could be delayed almost indefinitely, the relationship between the smallest and largest structural elements had become more and more ambiguous. Writing about the Second String Quartet, Schoenberg later observed that although in the third and fourth movements, where for the first time he gave up the convention of a key signature, 'the key is presented distinctly at all the main dividing points of the formal organization', nonetheless 'the overwhelming multitude of dissonances cannot be balanced any longer by occasional returns to such tonal triads as represent a key'.[1] If tonality was no longer fulfilling its primary organizational function, then the logic of the situation demanded that tonality be abandoned and that the nature of all those other musical elements that sprang from tonality be reassessed. This was the crucial step that Schoenberg took in 1908–09, and it was a step that Webern and Berg, both of whom had trodden the same path, took with him.

In the case of Berg, the borderline between tonality and free atonality was crossed in the last of the *Vier Lieder* (*Four Songs*), Op. 2, and the String Quartet, Op. 3, of 1910. In Berg's previous works, the Piano Sonata, Op. 1, and the first three of the *Vier Lieder*, a weakening of the sense of tonal direction had resulted from the use of harmonic and melodic formations based on the whole-tone scale and other tonally ambiguous interval structures. In these works, however, the tonally ambiguous elements were still integrated into a diatonic context. The last of the Op. 2 songs, on the other hand, makes no reference at all to traditional diatonic tonality.

Parallel to the evolution of his harmonic and melodic language in these early works runs the development of Berg's highly individual ideas on musical structure. Again the initial stimulus for these ideas can be found in the music which his teacher composed during and immediately after the period when Berg was studying with him. In the First Quartet, *Pelleas und Melisande,* and the First Chamber Symphony, Schoenberg had written works in which the separate movements of the traditional four-movement symphonic structure were welded into a single span. In the First Quartet, for example, the constituent sections of the traditional sonata-form movement are distributed throughout the work in such a way that the sonata exposition is separated from its first reprise by a scherzo, the first reprise from the development section by a slow movement, and the development from the final sonata recapitulation by a 'finale'. The whole is held together by a series of thematic interconnections and transformations: a subsidiary accompanying part may, for example, reappear as a main melodic idea, or a secondary theme in one movement may return as the main theme of another. This kind of thematic interconnection appears in Berg's first published work, the Piano Sonata, Op. 1, and is a consistent feature of all Berg's later music. The permanent influence which the formal innovations of these pre-atonal works of Schoenberg had upon his student can be seen in Berg's last work, the opera *Lulu,* in which the structural design of each act is dominated by a single large-scale form, the constituent parts of which are distributed throughout in the manner of Schoenberg's First Quartet. Though these formal and thematic techniques stem initially from Schoenberg, there is no precedent for the rigorously symmetrical and complex structural designs within which they are contained in Berg's mature work.

All the features mentioned above can already be seen in the set of five orchestral songs which Berg wrote in 1912, the *Altenberg Lieder,* Op. 4. Although each individual song is, in itself, extremely brief, with even the two outer and longest songs lasting no more than a few minutes each, the five songs are conceived as a single entity and are linked through a web of melodic, harmonic, and rhythmic motives of extraordinary complexity and subtlety. Each of the middle three songs of the cycle has a symmetrical arch-shape: the second half of Song II presents a compressed, retrograde statement of the harmonic and motivic progression of the first half; Song IV begins and ends with the same solo flute notes; at the centre, in Song III (which but for a change in verb tense begins and ends with the same line of text) a twelve-note chord that is gradually dismantled in the opening bars is reassembled in the closing bars. The symmetrical arch-shape of the individual songs is also a feature of the cycle as a whole, since the passacaglia theme of the last song has already appeared as the first main theme of Song I, while the harmonic progression which introduces the voice in the first song returns, in reverse, at the end of the whole work. Already evident in the Altenberg Songs are Berg's love of tightly organized formal structures, of textual symbols, of complex motivic interrelationships, as well as that feeling for broad dramatic gestures that were to characterize *Wozzeck*.

The first performance of the *Altenberg Lieder* was perhaps the greatest disaster of Berg's career. On 31 March 1913, Schoenberg performed the second and third songs of the cycle in a concert at the Musikvereinsaal in Vienna. The performance provoked one of the great scandals of twentieth-century music, a riot comparable only to that which greeted the first performance of *The Rite of Spring* in the same year. The experience proved so traumatic that Berg never again attempted to have the songs performed, and the *Altenberg Lieder* disappeared into an oblivion from which they were rescued only in 1952 when they received their first complete performance in Rome under Jascha Horenstein.

Although brief, neither the *Altenberg Lieder* nor the Four Pieces for Clarinet and Piano, Op. 5 which followed are aphoristic pieces of the kind that Webern was writing at the same time. Berg's natural lyricism and his instinct for dramatic gesture demanded a larger canvas. The essentially large-scale nature of his music becomes evident in the Three Orchestral Pieces, Op. 6, of 1913–15, the most overtly Mahlerian of all Berg's works. With this work, Berg, alone amongst the Second Viennese School at the time, confronted head-on the problems of creating large-scale, non-tonal musical structures.

The main thematic material of all three of the Op. 6 Pieces has its origin in the opening *Praeludium*, where there appear a number of small motivic figures – the most important being a three-note basic cell consisting of a minor third and a semitone – which, extended, inverted, or subjected to various registral displacements, pervade the whole work. Three more extended melodies in the *Praeludium* link all three movements. It is, however, extraordinarily difficult to give any kind of comprehensive survey of the thematic material of the Three Pieces.[2] As in the Five Orchestral Pieces, Op. 16, of Schoenberg, any aspect of a thematic idea – its pitch, interval structure, rhythm or contour – may serve as the starting point for another idea. The thematic transformations are complex and the number of new themes engendered so numerous that it is perhaps impossible to classify them, and in many cases certainly impossible to say which version of a theme represents its 'true' and which its 'varied' form.

In the second and third of the Op. 6 Pieces this web of thematic and motivic interrelationships is contained within the traditional forms and genres of their Mahlerian models – a rondo-like waltz in the second movement (*Reigen*) and a sonata-form (*Marsch*) in the third. The first movement, the *Praeludium*, does not employ a traditional formal structure but is designed as a movement away from and back to unpitched percussion sounds. The symmetrical arch-shape of this movement is underlined by the return of the opening chord sequence in retrograde at the end of the piece – one of the first examples of what was to become a constant feature of Berg's mature music. With the exception of the Violin Concerto (and the little twelve-note setting of 'Schliesse mir die Augen beide') all of Berg's compositions after the Three Orchestral Pieces include movements or scenes which either are framed by retrograde-related episodes as in the *Praeludium* or have large-scale palindromes at their centre. A further prophetic technique in the Op. 6 Pieces is the use of a rhythmic cell – what Berg himself was later to call 'a rhythm in the form of a motive'[3] – which is initially stated on a single reiterated note and which then appears in different melodic guises. Such rhythmic motives, which had played a small role in the *Vier Lieder*, Op. 2, and a more important role in the *Altenberg Lieder*, were to become increasingly important in Berg's later music.

The musical language of the Three Orchestral Pieces is essentially that of *Wozzeck* and, indeed, the two works are closely related to one another. His imagination fired by having seen the Büchner play, Berg began to make sketches for the opera immediately, while he was still working on the orchestral pieces. Some of the earliest sketches for *Wozzeck* appear on the same manuscript paper as sketches for the *Marsch* movement of Op. 6, and the two works even share thematic material in one case, bars 275–8 of Act I scene 2 of *Wozzeck* quoting bars 79–84 of the *Marsch*.

The main structural and technical features of the music which Berg wrote before *Wozzeck* can be summarized as follows:

(1) A love of precisely balanced symmetrical structures which often finds expression in complex arch-shaped designs and in large-scale palindromes.

(2) The view of a work as a single formal entity in which the individual movements or scenes are both self-contained structural elements and, at the same time, constituent parts of a single large-

scale design. Although the view of a work as a single entity is not in itself new (the different movements of a classical symphony are both self-contained formal designs and parts of a larger whole), Berg's larger structures differ from those of most of his predecessors in (a) the complexity of the web of thematic, harmonic, rhythmic, and – in the vocal works – textual cross-references which bind the movements together, and (b) the nature of the overall forms, which depend for their balance on the symmetries mentioned above. The ideal towards which Berg seems to have been striving in these early pieces, and which he achieved in *Wozzeck*, is of a work which exhibits both the greatest possible variety and differentiation between its different movements (each of which will have, as Berg himself said of *Wozzeck*, an 'unmistakable aspect, a rounded off and finished character'[4]) and, at the same time, the greatest possible overall formal and thematic unity.

(3) The use of rhythmic patterns as independent motives, i.e., as vehicles for various pitch-structures.

(4) The use of traditional forms within which operate the kind of thematic and formal techniques discussed in (1) and (2) above. Thus the final song of the *Altenberg Lieder* is a passacaglia which develops thematic and rhythmic material heard earlier in the cycle and which, as we have said above, completes the symmetrical arch-shape of the cycle as a whole. Similarly, the thematic material of the sonata-form *Marsch* of the Three Orchestral Pieces, Op. 6, has its origins in the two preceding pieces of the set.

(5) A tendency towards lyrical expansiveness and, even in the miniature pieces, large dramatic gestures – the glissandi and the reiterated low B♭ towards the end of the *Vier Lieder*, Op. 2, for example, or the moment at bar 35 of the last of the *Altenberg Lieder* when the orchestral crescendo is suddenly cut off to leave a high *pianississimo* A in the voice.

At first glance, Berg's use of rigourously symmetrical and predetermined formal structures and his use of independent rhythmic motives may suggest a somewhat theoretical and calculated approach to compositional technique. It is characteristic of Berg's music, however, that such apparently abstract procedures should produce music of an overwhelming emotional intensity. It is this seemingly paradoxical fusion of technical calculation and emotional spontaneity that gives Berg's music its peculiar fascination.[5]

Having sketched out a few ideas for *Wozzeck* in 1914, Berg was forced to put the project to one side. The immediate cause of his abandoning his work on the opera was the need to complete the still unfinished Three Orchestral Pieces, to finish his guide to the Schoenberg Chamber Symphony, and to deal with the administration of the Berg family's summer home in Carinthia. In July 1914 war was declared and the following summer Berg was called up for military service. After a short time at a training camp on the Austro-Hungarian frontier Berg was declared unfit for service in the field. He returned to Vienna and, in May 1916, took up a post in the War Ministry where he remained until the end of the war. Berg took up work on the opera again in 1917 but it was not until the late summer of 1918 that he was at last able to report to Webern that he was beginning to make progress on the piece, that he had finished one scene and hoped to complete another before his leave of absence was over.

Released from military service at the end of 1918, Berg was still unable to devote his time wholly to *Wozzeck*. In addition to the bread-and-butter work which he had to undertake to make a living – teaching, the preparation of further guides for the Viennese publishing firm Universal Edition, a brief spell of work as a musical journalist, and the constant work involved in supervising the family estate – Berg was also deeply involved in organizing and rehearsing concerts for Schoenberg's newly formed 'Verein für musikalische Privataufführungen' (Society for Private Musical Performances). Nevertheless, by July 1919 Act I of the opera was 'quite finished' along with 'one big scene' of Act II. The tavern garden scene (Act II scene 4) gave Berg particular difficulty and Act II was not completed until August 1921. Act III seems to have presented fewer problems, however, and the whole opera was completed in short score by mid October of 1921.

It was at this stage that Schoenberg saw the score of *Wozzeck* for the first time. He had at first opposed the idea of an opera on the subject and Berg had subsequently avoided showing him the work in progress. Schoenberg now wrote to Hertzka, the director of Universal Edition, his own principal publisher, recommending the work in glowing terms.

Berg began work on the full score of the opera while his pupil Fritz Heinrich Klein prepared a piano score. The full score was finally finished in April 1922 and a copy made in the following month. The piano score was completed in June of the same year. *Wozzeck* had, as yet, no commercial publisher and Berg borrowed money in order to pay for a private printing. The printing and proof corrections took up the final months of 1922 and the printed vocal score was at last ready in December 1922.

Berg now set about creating interest in the piece by advertising the publication and by sending copies of the score to opera companies and to critics likely to write about the work. The earliest mention of the opera in the press was in a short survey of the music of Webern and Berg in an article by their fellow Schoenberg pupil, Erwin Stein, but much more important was what Berg himself called a 'fabulous' article[6] by Ernst Viebig in the important Berlin periodical *Die Musik*. Devoted solely to *Wozzeck*, it included a reproduction of the Cradle Song of Act I scene 3. In the same month, April 1923, Berg signed a contract with Universal Edition, who took over the publication of *Wozzeck* and the Three Orchestral Pieces. Viebig's article created considerable controversy, provoking, in particular, a bitter attack on the work by the critic Emil Petschnig. (The articles, along with the reply which the Petschnig piece elicited from Berg, are reproduced in the final section of this book, on pp. 139–51.)

During the following months a number of opera companies made tentative approaches to Universal Edition about the opera but none of these enquiries resulted in any firm offers of a production of *Wozzeck*. Indeed, there seemed to be little reason why any established company should take the risk of mounting the first production of so difficult a work by a composer whose name was hardly known in his native Vienna and almost totally unknown in the outer world.

The turning point in Berg's fortunes came in August 1923 when the String Quartet, Op. 3, was performed at the ISCM (International Society for Contemporary Music) Festival in Salzburg. The first performance of the *Praeludium* and *Reigen* movements of the Op. 6 Pieces under Webern in Berlin two months earlier had met with a warm reception, but the Havemann Quartet's performance of Op. 3 at Salzburg proved to be the success of the Festival and brought Berg's music, for the first time, to the attention of the international musical community. The work was immediately taken up by other quartets and created considerable interest in Berg's other music. One outcome of the Salzburg performance was the suggestion by Hermann Scherchen, who had been in the audience, that Berg should make a concert suite from *Wozzeck*. The resulting *Drei Bruchstücke aus 'Wozzeck'* (*Three Fragments from 'Wozzeck'*) were first performed under Scherchen in Frankfurt in 1924. The performance was, as Berg reported to Webern, 'a great triumph with the public, the musicians, and the press'.[7]

By this time, however, Erich Kleiber had already declared his intention of performing the opera at the Berlin State Opera. Kleiber, a passionate admirer of the Büchner play, had already seen a piano score of the opera and, during the autumn of 1923, had made his interest in the piece known to a number of Berg's acquaintances. In January 1924 Kleiber was in Vienna for a few days and it was arranged, at his request, that the entire opera should be performed for him by the pianist Ernst Bachrich.[8] Berg, who was not an accomplished pianist, helped out in the more difficult parts of the score. By the time the first two scenes had been played Kleiber had already decided to do the work in Berlin, even if it were to cost him his job.[9]

The State Opera in Berlin was, at this time, passing through a particularly turbulent period in its history. The position of the general administrator, Max von Schillings, had long been insecure and was to become increasingly so as his relations with the Minister of Culture grew progressively worse during the spring and summer of 1925. Finally, in November 1925, Schillings openly defied the wishes of the Minister and was dismissed from his post three weeks before *Wozzeck* was scheduled to have its premiere. The dismissal galvanized every interested party – the press, the staff of the opera house and both the right- and left-wing political factions – into action. The liberal press denounced the dismissal as an unwarranted intervention by the bureaucracy into artistic affairs while the right wing used the affair as an opportunity to attack the policies of the new Republic.

Less than a fortnight before the premiere of the opera Berg was still not sure that it might not be cancelled. Schillings's dismissal had left his protégé Kleiber unprotected and, as Berg wrote in a letter to his wife on 6 December 1925, whether Kleiber stood or fell depended on the success of *Wozzeck*.[10]

Before even a note of *Wozzeck* had been heard, the opera – which happened to receive its premiere on the very day that the 'Schillings affair' came to a head with a debate in the Landstag – had become the focus of a bitter political dispute.[11]

4 Synopsis

(Although the formal and motivic structure of the opera is discussed in Chapter 5 the main formal units are indicated in square brackets in the following synopsis.)

Act I

Scene 1

The Captain's room; early morning

[Suite]

[Prelude: obbligato wind quintet] The curtain rises after three bars of music to reveal Wozzeck shaving the Captain. Pathologically afraid of the vast stretches of time which he sees lying before him, the Captain begs Wozzeck not to hurry, his first words 'Langsam, Wozzeck, langsam' ('Slowly, Wozzeck, slowly') filling in the tritone B♮–F♮ which will prove to have a fateful significance in the work as a whole. The Captain's opening words are introduced by a cor anglais theme that becomes particularly associated with him:

Ex. 1

'You've thirty years left to live', says the Captain. 'That's 360 months and who knows how many days and hours and minutes. What are you going to do with that vast expanse of time?' 'Jawohl, Herr Hauptmann', replies Wozzeck to the expressionless single-note figure of Ex. 2:

Ex. 2

[Pavane: bars 30ff, obbligato drums and harp] The tempo of the music changes as the Captain warms to the subject 'It makes me anxious for the world when I think of eternity' (the concept of eternity is symbolized in the orchestra by a fragment of the 'unending' cycle of fifths); 'it frightens me when I think that the world turns in a day, and whenever I see a millwheel I feel melancholy.' 'Jawohl, Herr Hauptmann', replies Wozzeck.

[Cadenza 1: obbligato solo viola] 'You always look so harassed. A good man doesn't rush around' says the Captain, whose obsession with time is only rivalled by his desire to present a solidly respectable image to the world.

[Gigue: bars 65ff, obbligato 3 flutes and celesta] Annoyed by his refusal to react to these philosophical musings the Captain begins to taunt Wozzeck, who, continuing to limit his replies to repetitions of 'Jawohl, Herr Hauptmann' (Ex. 2), agrees with everything – no matter how absurd – that the Captain says. Delighted by this proof of his batman's stupidity the Captain adopts the rhythm of Ex. 2 as he laughs at the humiliated batman.

[Cadenza 2: bar 109, obbligato solo double bass] 'You're a good man, Wozzeck, but you have no sense of morality', observes the Captain complacently.

[Gavotte: bars 115ff, obbligato brass] 'For example, you have an illegitimate child – a child "not blessed by the clergy" as the regimental chaplain says.' (The Captain here breaks into the deliberately bizarre falsetto which characterizes his vocal line; the orchestral accompaniment at this point imitates the sound of a church organ.) [Double 1: bars 127ff] 'The Lord will not think less of him for that', replies Wozzeck abandoning his submissive monotone for the first time. 'The Lord said "suffer the little children come to me".' [Double 2: bars 133ff] While the Captain, confused by this reply, is at a loss how to answer, Wozzeck, accompanied by the strings, finally gives vent to his feelings:

[Air: bars 136ff, obbligato strings] 'Poor folk like us, who have no money. . . I could be virtuous if I were a gentleman with a hat, and a watch and eyeglass.' Supported by the rhythm of his earlier 'Jawohl, Herr Hauptmann' and by the three superimposed diminished sevenths that together cover the complete chromatic collection, the words 'Poor folk like us' are set (Ex. 3) to what is perhaps the most important motive in the opera. The whole of this passage will return in the final orchestral interlude.

Ex. 3

Wir ar-me Leut!_

Alarmed by this unexpected outburst of emotion, the Captain attempts to calm Wozzeck down and restore their earlier relationship. [Postlude: bars 153ff] 'It's all right, you're a good fellow, Wozzeck', says the Captain soothingly, 'But you think too much. You're always so harassed.' (The phrases 'Ein guter Mensch' – 'a good fellow' and 'Er sieht immer so verhetzt aus' – 'you look so harassed' which have appeared earlier now reappear with their original setting.) As the conversation returns to topics treated earlier, the music with which the scene started (and the original wind quintet obbligato) reappears but in retrograde motion so that bars 157–70 correspond to bars 5–14 but backward. The larger implications of this detail will be discussed in Chapter 7. The immediate effect of the retrograde, however, is to ensure that the Captain's final words ('Off you go now – and go slowly, nice and slowly') are set to the notes to which these same words were set at the beginning of the scene.

Orchestral interlude

A contrapuntal development of the material of the first scene leads to an enormous *fortissimo* climax (over a pedal on Ex. 2) which is suddenly cut off as the curtain rises on:

Scene 2

An open field in the late afternoon. The town can be seen in the distance.

[Rhapsody]

Wozzeck and his friend and fellow soldier Andres are cutting kindling wood. Wozzeck is unsettled by the strange elemental forces which he feels in the natural world around him, by the sense of an alien, indifferent (perhaps even malevolent) nature, of a world in which the rising mists and the toadstool rings seem to be invested with a mysterious unfathomable significance. The strange haunted atmosphere of the scene is represented by the sequence of three chords shown in Ex. 4, the chords from which the rhapsody which is the formal basis of the scene develops.

Ex. 4

Andres, unaffected by the atmosphere of the place and by his friend's troubled hallucinations, sings a folksong but is interrupted by Wozzeck who hears noises beneath the ground. As the last rays of the setting sun suffuse the scene with a brilliant red light Wozzeck has a vision of the world engulfed by flames.

A distant drum roll recalls them to the barracks and the two men leave as darkness falls.

Orchestral interlude

The retreat (with clarinet imitating a bugle call) is sounded in the distance as the curtain slowly descends. Gently moving chords prolong the unnaturally still mood of the final bars of the scene until the atmosphere is broken by the sounds of a distant military band. The band gets gradually louder as the curtain rises on:

Scene 3

Marie's house: evening

[Military March and Lullaby]

Marie watches from her open window as the military band passes in the street beyond. Her neighbour Margret, also watching, comments upon Marie's evident admiration of the Drum Major.

Annoyed, Marie slams the window shut and turns to her child – the illegitimate child to whom the Captain referred in the first scene of the act. The sound of the on-stage military band stops abruptly, cut short by the closing of the window, and the pit orchestra announces the figuration shown in Ex. 5, a falling minor third–semitone figure accompanied by chords built of open fourths or fifths which progress by chromatic inflection.

Ex. 5

All of these characteristics are particularly associated with Marie's music; all are present in the opening phrase of the Lullaby that she now sings to the child:

Ex. 6

As Marie sinks into a reverie the music settles on to a characteristic static chord built of open fifths (the pitch shown in Ex. 7 below is almost as important a feature of the chord as the harmonic structure) which comes, in Berg's own words, to symbolize 'Marie's waiting':

Ex. 7

The lowest note of Ex. 7 sinks to B♮ (producing the fateful B–F tritone in the bass) and Marie's reverie is interrupted by a sudden knock on the window as Wozzeck pauses briefly on his way back to the barracks, his arrival announced – as are all his entrances or exits – by the motive shown in Ex. 8:

Ex. 8

He attempts to convey to Marie the strange feelings he experienced while cutting sticks in the field (his references to the earlier scene being accompanied by large-scale reprises of the music of Act I scene 2: compare, for example, the setting of his words 'There was a picture in the heavens and everything glowed' at bars 435–6 with the music of the setting sun at bars 289–93 of the previous scene). He glances briefly at the child before hurrying away (to the accompaniment of Ex. 8 inverted). Frightened, Marie rushes from the house.

Orchestral interlude

A development of Marie's minor third–semitone motive and its inversion leads (via the 'nature' chords of Ex. 4) to a distant reminiscence (viola, bar 483) of the introduction to the Military March with which Scene 3 began. Repeated on the clarinet with two of the notes changed, the march introduction becomes the twelve-note figuration shown in Ex. 9:

Ex. 9

Scene 4

The Doctor's study on a sunny afternoon

[Passacaglia]

Like the Captain, the Doctor is obsessed by the concept of time, but whereas the Captain is terrified by the idea of eternity, the Doctor hopes to triumph over eternity through scientific fame. For a small wage Wozzeck acts as a human guinea-pig on whom the Doctor can try out the bizarre dietary experiments which, he believes, will secure him immortality. Formally the scene is designed as a set of Passacaglia variations on the theme of Ex. 9 above. The twenty-one variations fall into three main groups.

In the first group (Variations 1–5) the Doctor questions Wozzeck to discover whether he has kept to his diet – 'Nothing but beans! Nothing but legumes! And next week mutton!', he tells his victim. But Wozzeck has failed him – he has been seen coughing in the street. (Berg here changed Büchner's 'gepisst' to the more refined – but dramatically meaningless – 'gehustet'.) The Doctor is angered by this betrayal but calms himself down since, as he says, 'Anger is unscientific.' 'I am quite calm. My pulse is beating its usual sixty', observes the Doctor as the metronome mark changes to crotchet = 60 to confirm this diagnosis.

A cantabile version of Wozzeck's entrance motive (Ex. 8) and of Ex. 7, as he remembers Marie, introduce the second group of variations (Variations 6–12), during which Wozzeck tells the Doctor of the feelings and visions he experienced while cutting sticks in the field. Much of the music of this section derives from that of scene 2. 'Have you seen the toadstools?', he asks the Doctor, 'Lines, circles, strange figures – if only one could read them.' Circular and palindromic figures in the accompanying instrumental parts hint at the mysterious patterns hidden in the toadstool rings. The final section begins (Variation 13) as the Doctor, pouncing on this unexpectedly revealed insight into Wozzeck's mental condition, declares that his patient is obsessed by an irrational *idée fixe*. The waltz melody to which he announces his diagnosis (and which will return in Act II when, with equally malicious glee, the Doctor diagnoses the Captain's condition also) is introduced by a new theme that will later reappear as a leitmotive associated with the Doctor:

Ex. 10

'You are suffering from an excellent aberatio [*sic*] mentalis partialis, second species', he declares as, with ever growing megalomania, he starts planning to explore this new field of scientific research.

Although the Doctor intends his remark about an 'aberatio mentalis partialis' to refer to Wozzeck's mental state, the music suggests that the words apply equally to that of the Doctor himself, since they are set to an expanding figure (Ex. 11) that looks back to that on the horn at bar 17 of the opening scene, thus drawing a musical parallel between the Captain's and the Doctor's mutual obsession with time.

Ex. 11

A further parallel between the two is drawn towards the end of the scene when, as the Doctor grows ever more ecstatic about his dreams of immortality, overlapping statements of the theme associated with his mania (Ex. 12) culminate in a chord composed entirely of superimposed perfect fourths – another form of the fragment of the 'unending' cycle of fifths which earlier, in the scene with the Captain, symbolized eternity.

Ex. 12

A final 'grandioso' peroration is abruptly checked as the Doctor takes himself in hand and resumes his earlier attitude of scientific detachment ('Wozzeck, show me your tongue again').

Orchestral interlude

Ascending statements of the final fragments of the Passacaglia theme (the same fragment that, descending, had introduced the previous scene) give way to what, in the following scene, becomes the music associated with the Drum Major's seduction of Marie. A quick curtain reveals:

Scene 5

The street before Marie's house. Evening twilight

[Rondo]

Marie is standing at her door admiring the Drum Major, who is posturing and boasting of his prowess. The Drum Major is accompanied by a figuration related to the earlier military music:

Ex. 13

The Drum Major attempts to embrace Marie. After struggling and initially repulsing him Marie gives in – 'Have it your own way, it's all the same.' The curtain falls slowly as the two disappear into the house.

Act II

Scene 1

Marie's room. Morning sunshine

[Sonata form]

The two alternating chords which closed Act I return as the curtain rises.
[Sonata exposition] Marie is sitting with the child on her lap. She is admiring, in a broken piece of mirror, the earrings which the Drum Major has given her. Because of its associations with the earrings at this point the accompanying orchestral theme (Ex. 14; the first subject of the Sonata exposition) acquires an important motivic significance as a symbol of Marie's guilt.

Ex. 14

The child stirs (bridge passage) and, turning to him, Marie sings (second subject) a lullaby – a macabre transformation of the Lullaby in Act I scene 3 – which threatens that the gipsies will carry him off unless he goes to sleep. (Coda) Frightened, the child hides his head in Marie's dress.

[Sonata exposition: first reprise] (First subject) Marie turns back to the mirror and to admiring the earrings. (Bridge passage) The child again sits up and (Second subject) Marie repeats her lullaby, this time pretending that the flickering reflection of the mirror on the wall is the sandman coming to take the child away. (Coda) Unseen, Wozzeck enters.

[Sonata development] Suddenly aware of Wozzeck's presence, Marie guiltily puts her hand to her ears to hide the earrings. Questioned by Wozzeck, she tells him that she has found the earrings in the street. 'I've never found anything like that', he observes, looking at the gold earrings, 'and two together.' He looks briefly at the child before giving Marie his wages from the Captain and the Doctor (it is at this point that there appears the prosaic C major triad mentioned in Berg's lecture on p. 163 below). He leaves.

[Sonata recapitulation] Ashamed, Marie's thoughts turn back to the earrings and her seduction by the Drum Major: 'I'm just a bad lot. Everything in this world goes to the devil – man, wife and child!'

Orchestral interlude

The curtain descends to a C major glissando. The rest of the recapitulation of the Sonata movement now continues in a purely orchestral form as the interlude between scenes 1 and 2.

Scene 2

A street in the town. Day

[Fantasia and fugue]

The curtain rises to an ascending C major scale on harp (mirroring the descending scale to which it fell at the beginning of the previous orchestral interlude.)

The Doctor, in a hurry, meets the Captain who detains him in conversation. 'No time! Must hurry', says the Doctor (the words 'Pressiert! Pressiert!' are set to the expanding 'aberatio mentalis' figure of Ex. 11) as the Captain assures him that 'a good man takes his time'.

The Captain is represented by the opening theme (Ex. 1) from Act I scene 1; the Doctor by one of the themes (Ex. 10) from Act I scene 5.

The Captain has become breathless in attempting to catch up with the Doctor and his breathing is now so laboured that it catches the Doctor's attention. Having described the details of some recent cases the Doctor turns to diagnosing (to the return of the waltz theme to which he earlier diagnosed Wozzeck) the Captain: 'bloated, fat, thick neck, apoplectic – you could easily have an apoplexia cerebra soon', he says with evident relish, 'it will be a fascinating case and will give rise to some wonderful experiments'.

Wozzeck enters and, from taunting each other, the Doctor and Captain turn to taunting him.

A triple fugue begins with the Captain's theme as the first subject, the Doctor's as the second and a new theme – derived from the coda theme of the previous scene's Sonata movement – representing Wozzeck. The Doctor and Captain hint, none too subtly, at Marie's unfaithfulness and her association with the Drum Major. Initially puzzled, Wozzeck suddenly realizes the implications of what they are saying and rushes off.

Orchestral interlude

A slow interlude for chamber orchestra anticipates the tempo, the orchestral texture and, in its references to the themes associated with the Drum Major, the musical material of the following scene.

Scene 3

The street before Marie's home. Overcast day

[Largo]

Marie is standing outside her door when Wozzeck arrives to confront her with his suspicions about her infidelity.

The scene is scored for chamber orchestra (an orchestra with – as a homage to Berg's teacher at this, the central point of the opera – an identical layout to that of Schoenberg's First Chamber Symphony). The full orchestra makes only occasional contributions.

Although Marie pretends not to understand Wozzeck's accusations, the musical material, which consists almost entirely of quotations from the music of the seduction scene and the earlier Military March, makes it clear that she is well aware of his meaning.

Finally, losing his control, Wozzeck rushes to strike Marie. 'Don't touch me', cries Marie (to the musical figuration to which these same words were set in her struggle with the Drum Major in Act I). 'Better a knife in my heart than dare to lay a hand on me.' As she says these words the chromatic wedge figuration that will come to symbolize the murder weapon appears for the first time:

Ex. 15

Wozzeck, frightened by the prospect which these words suddenly open up, leaves.

Orchestral interlude

The gently undulating music which introduced the previous scene returns and, working its way backwards (cf. bars 406–11 and bars 368–62) gradually turns into the slow Ländler which forms the interlude and becomes the main material for the following scene.

Scene 4

A tavern garden. Late evening

[Scherzo with two trios]

A group of soldiers, apprentices and girls are passing the evening in a tavern garden. Some are dancing to the accompaniment of an on-stage band (a typical *heuriger* band of the kind that Berg would have heard playing in the local Viennese taverns).

Two apprentices sing rambling monologues before they fall into a drunken stupor and the company, now including Marie and the Drum Major, returns to the dance floor. The seduction music of Act I scene 5, now transformed into a waltz, reappears as Marie dances with the Drum Major. Wozzeck enters and watches them.

The dancing is interrupted firstly by the singing of a hunting chorus, then by a song from Andres, and finally by another monologue from one of the drunken apprentices.

As the band retunes, a simpleton enters and crosses over to Wozzeck. Like the idiot in Mussorgsky's *Boris Godunov* the simpleton has the ability to see into the future. 'Everyone is happy', he says, 'but it stinks of blood'. The word 'blood' lodges itself in Wozzeck's mind and the scene before him suddenly seems to be bathed in a blood-red mist.

Orchestral interlude

The dance music, becoming ever more distorted and frantic, continues after the fall of the curtain until it is suddenly cut off, leaving only the sound of a men's chorus singing the 'nature music' which opened Act I scene 2.

Scene 5

The guard room in the barracks. Night

[Introduction and rondo]

The curtain slowly rises on the dormitory in the barracks and the wordless nature chorus is revealed as being the sounds of the sleeping soldiers. Wozzeck wakes suddenly, tormented by the memory of the previous tavern scene. He hears voices speaking to him from the wall (the music here refers back to that of Act I scene 2 when he heard noises beneath the ground) and has a vision of a flashing knife-blade.

His attempts at prayer (again set to music heard earlier in Act I scene 2) are interrupted as the drunken Drum Major staggers in, boasting noisily of his conquests. The music of Marie's struggle with the Drum Major in Act I scene 5 returns as Wozzeck and the Drum Major fight and Wozzeck is knocked to the ground. The two alternating chords which closed Act I (and opened Act II) fade away leaving only a low B♮ – the note that will dominate the murder scene – on the harp.

Act III

Scene 1

Marie's room. Night. Candlelight

[Invention on a theme]

Overcome by guilt, Marie is reading the story of the woman taken in adultery from the Bible. Upset, the child presses himself to her and she tells him a fairy story before returning to the Bible and reading about Mary Magdalene.

Orchestral interlude

The variation theme of the previous scene is further developed by the orchestra and dies away as a glacial arpeggio on harp and celesta introduces the note B♮, the note which runs throughout the following scene.

Scene 2

A forest path by a pool. Dusk

[Invention on a note]

Marie and Wozzeck are walking through the wood. Anxious, Marie tries to hurry on but Wozzeck detains her. A disjointed, sinister conversation follows until, as the moon rises, blood-red, Wozzeck draws a knife. A long crescendo begins as the note B♮, which has been present as a subdued pedal point throughout the scene, is now taken up by the kettledrums. Wozzeck plunges the knife into Marie's throat. A brief, nightmarish version of all the main musical motives associated with Marie is heard in the orchestra and she falls to the ground dead. Marie's waiting motif (Ex. 7), with the fateful B–F tritone in the bass, and the inverted form of Wozzeck's entrance motive (Ex. 8) appear as he leaves.

Orchestral interlude

An enormous crescendo on the note B♮, the note which has dominated the murder scene, is interrupted by a *fortissimo* chord (the chord on which Scene 4 will be built) and a rhythm pounded out on the bass drum. A second crescendo on B♮, this time played by the whole orchestra, is suddenly cut off as the curtain rises on:

Scene 3

A low, badly lit tavern. Night

[Invention on a rhythm]

A coarse polka, badly played on an out-of-tune piano, is heard as Wozzeck, trying to forget what has just happened, is discovered drinking in a low tavern. The rhythm of the polka melody, which is the rhythmic pattern that dominates the whole scene, is a version of that heard on the bass drum in the previous interlude.

Shouting down the pub pianist, Wozzeck begins to sing a folk song, but the words and the music are too reminiscent of Marie (the melody of the song is a further variant of the Lullaby of Act I) and he leaves it unfinished. He persuades Margret to sing but is again reminded of earlier events and stops her. Margret notices the blood on Wozzeck's hand and, refusing to believe Wozzeck's excuse, she attracts the attention of the other customers in the tavern. Wozzeck rushes off, panic-stricken.

Orchestral interlude

Superimposed statements of the dominant rhythmic pattern of the previous scene lead to a quickly suppressed climax.

Scene 4

The forest path by the pool. Night

[Invention on a six-note chord]

Wozzeck returns to the scene of the crime to recover the murder weapon. He stumbles over Marie's corpse. Discovering the knife he throws it into the pool. As he does so the blood-red moon breaks through the clouds. 'The moon betrays me. The knife is too near the shore, they'll discover it', he says, wading into the pool to throw the knife further. In the red moonlight he imagines that he is covered in blood. He wades further into the pool, trying to wash himself clean in the blood-red water, and drowns. As he does so the Doctor and the Captain pass by and hurry away, determined not to become involved in something which is no concern of theirs. As the drowning music fades away the croaking of the toads around the pool, heard briefly at the beginning of the scene, returns – the sounds of the indifferent natural world which continue unaffected by the human tragedy that has taken place.

Orchestral interlude

[Invention on a key]

The final *Adagio* orchestral interlude, the emotional focus of the whole opera, begins – a recapitulation and summing up of all the main musical motives in the work (other than those associated with Marie, which will appear in the final scene) and a threnody for the dead Wozzeck.

The final bars of the interlude, as the music returns to the tonic D minor, give way to an icy arpeggio figuration which leads to:

Scene 5

In front of Marie's house. Bright morning sunlight

[Invention on a constant quaver figuration]

In stark contrast to the intense emotional atmosphere of the previous interlude the final scene of the opera returns us to the cold unfeeling everyday world. Marie's child is playing with other children in the street. A small child enters with news of the discovery of Marie's body and the children run off to look. After being left alone for a moment Marie's child follows his playmates. A final statement of the motives associated with Marie leads to a return of the undulating chords which closed the earlier acts and with which the whole opera now ends.

5 The formal design

The documents reprinted in the final section of this book give some idea of the extent to which even the earliest reviewers and commentators on *Wozzeck* – and, indeed, even those commentators who wrote in advance of the first performance – concentrated their attention on the unusual formal design of the work.

Berg was later to suggest (in 'A word about "Wozzeck"', reprinted on p. 152) that the interest in this one aspect of the piece was excessive, that it was an interest that sprang from the critics themselves ('so much has been written that I can hardly say anything without plagiarizing my critics') and that he himself 'never entertained' the idea of reforming the formal structure of opera. Such suggestions seem disingenuous, if not downright dishonest, in view of the fact that many of the earliest articles on the opera were written by the composer's own pupils or colleagues, and that he himself ensured that a chart of the formal design of the piece was included in all the copies of the 1923 vocal score sent to the critics. This chart, prepared by Berg's pupil Fritz Mahler – probably made at the suggestion, and certainly done with the authority, of the composer himself – is well known to all students of the work and is reproduced on p. 42.

As Mahler's chart shows, *Wozzeck* consists of three acts of five scenes each; each act, and each scene within each act, is designed as a self-contained musical structure. The expository Act I, in which each scene introduces one of the five other figures in the drama, is designed as a sequence of five character-pieces. The central Act II is designed as a five-movement symphony, while Act III forms a series of five inventions, with a sixth 'invention on a key' forming the big orchestral interlude between the last two scenes. The overall plan of the opera is, therefore, that of a large arch-structure, the three acts together forming what Berg himself described as a traditional three-part ABA structure with the two more loosely-constructed outer acts framing the 'much larger and weightier middle act symmetrically'.

Wozzeck: Dramatic and musical structure

Drama		Music
	ACT I	
Expositions		Five character pieces
Wozzeck in relation to		
his environment		
Wozzeck and the Captain	Scene 1	Suite
Wozzeck and Andres	Scene 2	Rhapsody
Wozzeck and Marie	Scene 3	Military March
		and Lullaby
Wozzeck and the Doctor	Scene 4	Passacaglia
Marie and the Drum Major	Scene 5	Andante affettuoso
		(quasi Rondo)
	ACT II	
Dramatic development		Symphony in five
		movements
Marie and her child,	Scene 1	Sonata movement
later Wozzeck		
The Captain and the	Scene 2	Fantasia and fugue
Doctor, later Wozzeck		
Marie and Wozzeck	Scene 3	Largo
Garden of a tavern	Scene 4	Scherzo
Guard room in the barracks	Scene 5	Rondo con introduzione
	ACT III	
Catastrophe and epilogue		Six inventions
Marie and her child	Scene 1	Invention on a theme
Marie and Wozzeck	Scene 2	Invention on a note
A low bar	Scene 3	Invention on a rhythm
Death of Wozzeck	Scene 4	Invention on a hexachord
	Orchestral interlude: invention on a key	
Children playing	Scene 5	Invention on a regular
		quaver movement

The relationship between the two outer acts is emphasized in a number of ways, most noticeably, perhaps, by the correspondence between the two most striking visual images in the opera – the setting of the red sun in Act I and, its 'retrograde inversion', the rising of the blood-red moon in Act III.

Within this large-scale plan, the musical forms chosen for the individual scenes are, of course, determined by dramatic considerations. In some scenes the musical material is of a kind that is traditionally associated with the kind of activity depicted on stage – the military march and lullaby of Act I scene 3, for example, or the ländler and waltz of the tavern scene (Act II scene 4) and the piano polka of the pub scene of Act III scene 3. In other scenes the musical form has a symbolic significance, representing the dramatic or the psychological kernel of the scene. In the final act, for example, the various obsessions which dominate Wozzeck's thoughts are symbolized in single musical elements which dominate each of the three scenes in which he is present. Thus, in the murder-scene of Act III scene 2 (the 'Invention on a note') the extent to which the ever-present B♮ recedes into or emerges from the musical texture reflects the extent to which the idea of murder fluctuates in Wozzeck's mind, finally coming to the fore only at the moment when he draws the knife and stabs Marie. The orchestral interlude that follows this scene consists of two crescendos on the note B♮ separated by a *fortissimo* drum statement of the rhythm that will form the basis of the next scene. In the pub scene that follows the constant presence of this one rhythmic pattern stands as a striking and effective symbol of Wozzeck's suppressed consciousness of this crime, while the individual statements of the rhythm, adapting themselves to the moment-to-moment contingencies of the text, mirror the hesitations and the unpredictable outbursts of Wozzeck and the accusations of Margret and the chorus. The obsessive musical element of the drowning scene of Act III scene 4, the scene discussed in some detail in the following chapter, is a single chord. In the final scene the constant moto-perpetuo quaver movement represents the ordinary matter-of-fact world of the children, a world that is hardly disturbed by the discovery of Marie's body and the revelation of what has occurred.

The separate juxtaposed movements of the suite of Act I scene 1 form (as Berg himself observes in his lecture on the opera) a fitting musical parallel to the way in which the conversation between the Captain and Wozzeck jumps from one topic to another. Less obviously, the choice of baroque (that is to say, 'old-fashioned') dance-forms is also a comment on the Captain's out-dated, traditional and bourgeois moral stance. Berg uses baroque forms with the same symbolic associations in *Lulu*, where Dr Schoen's desire for respectability is represented by a musette and gavotte.

A similarly esoteric use of such formal symbolism marks the scene with the Doctor (Act I scene 4) where the recurrent passacaglia theme is both a symbol of the Doctor's own recurrent *idée-fixe* (his dream of achieving immortal fame through the results of his bizarre dietary experiments) and, since the passacaglia is usually regarded as being a particularly 'learned' or 'scholarly' form of musical composition, an ironic comment on the Doctor's own scholarly pretensions.

As both composer and librettist Berg was able to ensure that the musical forms employed not only reflected the overall dramatic or psychological shape of the individual scenes but also that they provided a precise musical parallel to the forms defined by the text.

Thus, while the choice of a triple fugue for Act II scene 2 was determined by the general nature of the scene – in which each of the three characters involved pursues his own private obsession – the detailed working-out of the three fugue subjects is also an exact reflection of the moment-to-moment demands of the text and stage action. Each character in turn has a short monologue (which, musically, serves as the exposition of the fugue subject associated with that character) after which the course of the fugal development is completely determined by the course of the text, each subject appearing only at the point at which the character associated with it is singing or is directed to perform an action. The correlation between music and text is so precise that even the smallest detail of the stage action (as, for example, the moments when the Captain is directed to tap his forehead) are drawn into the musical structure of the scene.

Act II scene 1, like Act II scene 2, also involves three characters, although in this case, as Berg himself pointed out, the three characters – Marie, Wozzeck and the child – have a family relationship. Again, the musical form employed is a precise reflection of the textual and dramatic structure of the scene. Musically the scene is designed as a sonata-form movement in which the exposition is repeated, as in a classical symphony. The first subject of the sonata accompanies Marie as she admires, in a piece of broken mirror, the earrings which the Drum Major has given her. The bridge passage begins as she turns her attention to the restless child, and the song which she sings to him as she attempts to frighten him into going to sleep forms the second subject. A short coda closes this first statement of the sonata exposition.

The repetition of the exposition – not a literal restatement as in the classical symphony – begins as Marie turns back to the mirror. It continues as the original sequence of events (the stirring of the child and Marie's attempts to frighten him into sleeping) repeats itself. Wozzeck unexpectedly enters to the reprise of the original coda theme, which now becomes associated with him.

The development section, the point of highest musical tension, coincides with the point of highest dramatic tension in the scene, as Wozzeck questions Marie about her 'discovery' of the earrings. He then gives Marie his wages from the Captain and the Doctor and leaves. The sonata recapitulation starts and continues through the descent of the curtain to form the following orchestral interlude. It is a restatement of the expository thematic elements, much intensified so as to reflect Marie's disturbed state after Wozzeck's departure.

Berg's use of the forms of 'absolute' instrumental music in an opera, and his handling of these forms in such a way that the apparently 'abstract' musical structure enhances a developing dramatic situation, is not without precedent. Many similar examples can be found in Mozart's operas. In *Wozzeck*, however, the musical constituents of these forms acquire an added significance by virtue of their additional roles as elements in the complex system of leitmotives and recapitulatory episodes which runs throughout the work. Thus, the first subject of the sonata form of Act II scene I, which on its first appearance is associated with the earrings, subsequently, because of this original association, functions as a leitmotive symbolizing Marie's guilt. Similarly, the sonata bridge passage, which is originally associated with the child, returns in the other two scenes of the opera in which the child appears: the Bible-reading scene of Act III and, as the basis of the harmonic structure, in the closing scene. Since Marie has already sung a lullaby to the child in Act I scene 3, the song to the child in Act II scene 1, the second subject of the sonata movement, is itself a thematic transformation of the earlier lullaby. The same melody will return, as a distant memory, at the end of the opera. The coda theme to which Wozzeck enters in Act II scene 1, will become the basis of his fugue subject in the triple fugue of the following scene. The other two subjects in this fugue have also been heard earlier in the opera – that associated with the Captain as one of the main themes of Act I scene 1, and that associated with the Doctor in Act I scene 4, respectively the only scenes in which the Captain and the Doctor have heretofore appeared.

The relationship between the theme of the coda of the sonata movement of Act II scene 1, and Wozzeck's fugue subject of Act II scene 2, illustrates a particular feature of the leitmotivic structure of the opera. As Ex. 16 shows, the coda theme (Ex. 16a) and the fugue subject (Ex. 16b) are not identical; they are distinct, separate themes related to one another through a common pitch collection (the whole-tone content of Ex. 16a is repeated, transposed, in a segment, marked *x*, of Ex. 16b), through rhythmic similarities, and through similarities of contour and instrumentation (both themes are originally played by the trombones). The total content of Wozzeck's fugue subject, which can be reduced to the scale of five whole-tones and a semitone shown in Ex. 17, is a collection that links many of the most important themes of the opera.

Ex. 16

Ex. 17

Most of the leitmotives in *Wozzeck* are themes that have a clear melodic and rhythmic shape and that are immediately recognizable when they recur. On occasion, however, some of these themes are transformed in such a way that their melodic and rhythmic identities are destroyed. In such cases the link between the different versions of a leitmotive is their common relative pitch content – that is to say that the different versions define the same harmonic unit. The first subject of the sonata movement of Act II scene 1 is one such leitmotive. On its original appearance the first phrase of the sonata's first subject takes the following form:

Ex. 18

A slightly varied version of this theme, in which the first four notes and their accompanying chords are transposed up a semitone, appears amongst the other leitmotives associated with Marie at the moment of her death:

Ex. 19

Reordered to form the ascending five-note collection shown in Ex. 20, the first phrase of the sonata movement becomes a symbol of Marie's guilt, appearing (transposed up a fourth) later in Act I scene 3, to the words 'Bin ich ein schlecht Mensch?' ('Am I a wicked person?') and, in retrograde, to the words 'Ich bin doch ein schlecht Mensch' ('I am a wicked person') (Ex. 21a and b).

Ex. 20

Ex. 21

The same phrase is recalled in Act III scene 3, when Wozzeck cries out, as his accusers crowd around him, 'Bin ich ein Mörder?' ('Am I a murderer?'):

Ex. 22

The leitmotive returns in the following scene as Wozzeck, searching for the knife, sees Marie's body, her cut throat 'earned, like the earrings, by her sin':

Ex. 23

Wie die Ohr - ring-lein   mit Deiner   Sün - de!

In the passage shown in Ex. 23 this five-note 'guilt' motive takes a form and is at a pitch level that identifies it with the final phrase of Marie's lullaby to the child in Act I scene 3, a relationship that is one link in a whole chain of relationships that connect some of the most important leitmotives in the opera. The first five notes of the final phrase of the lullaby (the five notes that are separated by a crotchet's rest from the remaining three notes) are an inversion of the five-note 'guilt' motive discussed above.

Ex. 24

Lau - ter   küh - le   Wein   muss   es   sein!

In both the 'guilt' motive and the lullaby these five notes are, characteristically, presented as a chain of thirds. It is this spacing that links the first four notes of the final phrase of the lullaby and the 'guilt' motive with the most important leitmotive in the opera, the leitmotive which, through its original association with the words 'Wir arme Leut' ('Poor folk like us'), comes to represent the poverty, and consequently the social conditions, which eventually precipitate the final tragedy:

Ex. 25

When, in Act II scene 4, the Fool first mentions the word 'blood', Wozzeck repeats the word to a transposed version of the four-note collection shown in Ex. 25 (an E♭ minor chord with added major seventh) which is then taken up and obsessively repeated by the orchestra:

Ex. 26

Blut?   Blut, Blut   Mir wird rot   vor   den   Au - gen

The appearance of this chord at this pitch level here (and its re-appearance at the same pitch level later in the opera) is especially significant since, as Ex. 27 shows, it is at this level that the four notes of this collection (again with the characteristic spacing) appear in the leitmotive associated with Wozzeck himself:

Ex. 27

The relationship between the murder of Marie (symbolically projected by the 'blood' chord), poverty (symbolized by the 'Wir arme Leut' motive), and Wozzeck and Marie is, in this way, already implicit in the relationship between their associated leitmotives.

Not only leitmotives but also larger musical units reappear during the course of the opera. In most cases these musical repetitions are occasioned by textual reminiscences, as a character recalls or describes something that has happened earlier in the opera. Thus large-scale repetitions of the music of Act I scene 2 accompany Wozzeck's later attempts to describe to Marie (in Act I scene 3) and the Doctor (in Act I scene 4) his experiences while cutting kindling wood in the fields. Similarly when, in Act II scene 3, Wozzeck confronts Marie with his supicions of her infidelity, his accusations are accompanied by repetitions of the music which was earlier associated with the Drum Major and of the music of the seduction scene of Act I scene 5.

Elsewhere in the opera large sections of music return not because the characters themselves conciously refer to an earlier event but because their words suggest some kind of link with what has happened before or because the composer wishes to point out a relationship between two seemingly unrelated incidents. When in Act III scene 3, bars 180–2, for example, Wozzeck cries 'Nein! Keine Schuh, man kann auch blossfüssig in die Höll' geh'n!' ('No! No shoes! One can also go barefoot to hell!') his words are accompanied by a repetition of the music of bars 597–8 in Act II scene 4, the music which originally occurred as the setting of the words 'Es sind manche Leut' nah an der Tür und wissen's nicht, bis man sie zur Tür hinaus trägt, die Füss' voran' ('There are many people near the door and don't know it until they're carried out feet first').

Amongst the associations imposed by Berg himself is that between the opening of Act II scene 5, as the soldiers lie sleeping in the barracks, and the 'nature' sounds of Act I scene 2, the scene in the open field, and also that between Wozzeck's fight with the Drum Major in the last scene of Act II and Marie's struggle with the Drum Major in the last scene of the first act.

A particularly telling recapitulation is the return of bars 261–5 of Act II scene 2 as part of the final orchestral interlude. In their first appearance, in Act II, these bars form a mock funeral march as the Captain, terrified by the Doctor's predictions that he will suffer a stroke in the immediate future, self-pityingly imagines the mourners following his coffin. On their reappearance in the D minor orchestral interlude these same bars are, with bitter irony, transformed into a real funeral march for the now dead Wozzeck.

The formal structure of *Wozzeck* cannot be discussed in terms of the musical design alone, however, for, as George Perle has pointed out, 'the purely visual and non-musical aspects of the production, spelled out in the most extraordinary detail by the composer, play an integral role in the overall design to a degree that has no parallel in operatic composition before Berg.'[1]

The already-mentioned visual parallel between the setting sun of Act I scene 2 and the rising moon of Act III scene 2 is one example of the way in which the non-musical elements underline, and draw attention to, the large-scale design of the work, while, on a smaller scale, we have already demonstrated not only the way in which the textual and musical plan of such scenes as Act II scenes 1 and 2 are so interdependent as to be inseparable but also the way in which the most detailed aspects of the production are mapped into this musical and textual structure.

The way in which Berg incorporates the curtain into the formal design of the opera is particularly ingenious. As Perle has again observed, while some curtains such as those that end Act II scene 1 and open Act II scene 2 are synchronized with special curtain music (as 'irrelevant to the staged events as the architectural ornament that decorates the proscenium'), 'the rise and fall of every curtain, even when it is not accompanied by special curtain music, is "composed" in terms of extra-musical as well as musical correspondences and is thus an integral component of the overall design.'[2] At the end of Act II, for example, the action finishes with Wozzeck, thrashed by the Drum Major, staring blankly before him as the music ends with the low B♮ that looks forward to the murder scene of the next act. But the curtain does not fall immediately. Instead there are two bars without music during which we are presented with a 'stage picture' of the defeated Wozzeck. The curtain then falls in silence. At the beginning of Act III a similarly silent curtain presents a stage picture (both the rise of the curtain and the stage picture itself being of exactly the same duration as those that ended the previous act) of Marie reading the Bible. Perle has remarked on how 'this "delayed" fall and "premature" rise of the curtain prolong the audience's view of the stage world beyond its "proper" time' and how 'the opposite effect (a "prematurely" dropped curtain) is used to heighten the conclusion of Act III, sc. 3'.[3]

In a similar way the grotesque curtain that closes Act I scene 4 – falling 'at first quickly and then suddenly slowly, and at last quite gradually' – reflects the 'sudden change in the Doctor's behaviour at the conclusion of the scene when he becomes "suddenly quite calm" as he begins his examination of Wozzeck'. 'Through the composer's instructions for the manipulation of the curtain', comments Perle, 'the ambiguous relation between the "real" world of the spectators and the fictional world on the stage becomes a component of the work itself.' In every case the speed at which the curtain falls or rises is determined and precisely indicated in the score. Sadly, few producers of the opera show as sophisticated and subtle an understanding of Berg's musico-dramatic techniques as does George Perle or feel it necessary to observe those directions that will realize Berg's carefully worked-out correlation between what is happening on stage and what is happening in the orchestra pit.

In addition to overt musical and dramatic relationships of the kind discussed in the present chapter, the formal design of *Wozzeck* has also hidden within it a number of less obvious musical/textual relationships – relationships that are so idiosyncratic in nature and so consistently exploited in the work itself that one is forced to the conclusion that Berg himself regarded them as having a special, and very personal, significance. Chapter 7 discusses, and speculates on the symbolic significance of these more esoteric relationships and, on the basis of this discussion, suggests a possible interpretation of the opera.

6 *Act III scene 4: an analysis*

Act III scene 4 – the scene in which Wozzeck meets his death – is designed as an invention on a single six-note chord, the hexachord shown in Ex. 28 below. Before the opening of Act III scene 4 this chord has appeared only once in the work, at bar 114 of Act III, when a *fortissimo* statement of this hexachord cut off the first of the two crescendos on B♮ which form the orchestral interlude between scenes 2 and 3 of the act.

Ex. 28

Ex. 28 shows the chord at its original and most important pitch level, a level that we shall call 'T⁰' – that is, 'Transposition 0'. In the rest of this chapter the number after the letter 'T' will indicate the number of semitones above T⁰ at which a transposition of this chord appears. Ex. 28 also illustrates the vertical spacing that character-izes the chord on its first appearance, a spacing that returns as a point of reference at a number of places throughout the scene.

In the context of Act III as a whole the hexachord upon which scene 4 is based forms one step in a large-scale chromatic progres-sion. This progression, starting with the chord with which the preceding orchestral interlude ends at bar 219, gradually focuses onto the D minor chord that opens the final orchestral interlude:

Ex. 29

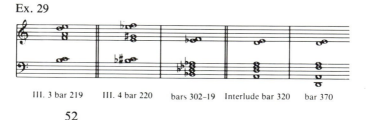

III. 3 bar 219   III. 4 bar 220   bars 302–19   Interlude bar 320   bar 370

52

Musically and dramatically the scene can be divided into three main sections. In every case significant changes in the handling of the hexachord coincide with and mark out the crucial dramatic points in the scene.

Part One: bars 220–66: Wozzeck searches for the knife

Having rushed away from the pub at the end of the previous scene, Wozzeck returns to the woodland path where he killed Marie to recover the murder weapon. He stumbles over Marie's body, finds the incriminating knife and throws it into the nearby pond.

Throughout this first section the six-note chord of Ex. 28 is used exclusively at its original pitch level (T^0). The whole section is framed by two almost identical statements of the original chord. The scene opens (bars 220–2) with repeated statements of the hexachord at the level and with the spacing shown in Ex. 28; the same repeated chord returns, two octaves lower, at the end of the first section (bars 257–64) as Wozzeck throws the knife into the pond.

The placing of the note F♮ as the highest note of this characteristic form of the chord has a particular significance. The B♮ component of the B–F tritone, the 'fate dyad' that plays so important a role in the work as a whole, has, of course, dominated the scene of Marie's death – the 'Invention on a note'. There is an allusion to the symbolic importance of this note at bar 232 of the present scene when Wozzeck sings the word 'tot' ('dead') on a B♮ – a note that does not appear in the hexachord. The complimentary F♮, the other note of the 'fate' tritone, now dominates Wozzeck's death scene; notice, for example, the way in which the B♮ of 'tot' at bar 232 is immediately followed by a high F♮ (the highest note of the vocal part throughout the scene) on the word 'Mörder' ('murder') at bars 233–4.

Within the forty-six-bar section defined by these 'framing' statements of the hexachord in its most characteristic form, a sense of harmonic variety is achieved by varying the disposition of the chord layout, by octave transposition of different segments of the chord and by emphasizing the different intervals that can be extracted from this six-note collection. At bars 226–30, for example, the woodwind ostinati, which represent the croaking of the toads around the pool, draw attention to the two adjacent semitones (F–E, E–D♯) contained in the collection, while the chord sustained by the strings in the following bars (bars 230–2) emphasizes the interval of a minor third. Similarly the horn and trombone figures at bars 234–5 emphasize whole tones, while the chords on the first beat of bar 241 and the second beat of bar 255 are composed of perfect fourths. The interval of a minor third (there are three different minor thirds embodied in the hexachord) acquires a particular importance during the scene because of its association with the words 'Das Messer' ('the knife') – the words heard in the opening bars of the scene where they are accompanied by a repeated minor third on the notes B♭–D♭ on the timpani. The B♭–D♭ minor third returns on the timpani at the very end of the scene when it leads into the following orchestral interlude. Although the words 'Das Messer' are spoken rather than sung in these opening bars Berg nonetheless notates these spoken words on the pitches B♭–D♭. In this first section of the scene the B♭–D♭ third reappears prominently in the vocal part at bars 227, 235, 239, 240, 244 and, to the repeated cries of 'Mörder', at bars 249–51 of this section. The words 'Das Messer' return on one of the alternative minor thirds (A–C) at bars 253–4 ('The knife will betray me'). In the following section the minor third B–D appears at bar 270, as Wozzeck realizes that the knife is lying too close to the edge of the pool, and as he wades into the pool to search for the weapon (bar 274: 'I can't find it').

With the exception of a few notes in the vocal line, a chord in the brass at bar 251 that consists of notes not included in the original hexachord, and a number of leitmotives that are superimposed upon this otherwise self-contained harmonic background, almost all the notes in this first section of the scene are derived from the six-note chord at T⁰. Amongst the leitmotives and the other references to music heard earlier in the opera which appear in this section are:

(1) A reference to the chromatic 'knife leitmotive' in the chain of chromatically descending minor ninths when Wozzeck first enters at bars 222–5;

(2) The already-mentioned appearance of the note B♮ on the word 'tot' at bar 232;

(3) The return of the on-stage Waltz music of Act II scene 4 (compare Act III scene 4, bar 241–3 and Act II scene 4, bars 480ff) as Wozzeck remarks on the cut across the throat of Marie's corpse ('What is that red band around your neck?'). At the pitch at which it appears here in Act III scene 4 the Waltz music also includes references to the Drum Major's motive, to the main pitches of Marie's 'waiting motive' (the notes B–C–F–E and A which begin the Waltz melody at bar 241) and to the E♭ minor chord that was earlier (Act II scene 4, bars 668–78) associated with the word 'blood'.

(4) A reference to the first subject of the Sonata movement of

Act II scene 1 – the theme that, through its association with the earrings, has become a symbol of Marie's infidelity – in the collection of notes to which are set Wozzeck's words 'Was that red necklace, like the earrings, earned by your sin?' The reappearance of this collection at this point has already been discussed and illustrated in the previous chapter.

The opening six-note chord returns to its original spacing at the end of the Part One (bars 257ff) as Wozzeck throws the knife into the pond. As he does so the blood-red moon breaks through the clouds, an appearance marked by ascending statements of the hexachord divided into two-note segments as shown in Ex. 30. The appearance of the moon precipitates a further development in Wozzeck's increasing madness and the second part of the scene begins.

Ex. 30

Part Two: bars 267–302: Wozzeck wades into the pool and drowns

Thinking that the knife might still be discovered, Wozzeck wades into the pond to find it. The red moonlight leads him to imagine that he is covered in blood and, trying to wash himself clean in water that itself appears to be a blood red, he drowns.

The second part of the scene begins as the ascending dyads of the 'moon music' at bars 264–6 give way to descending dyads derived from the six-note chord transposed a minor third higher to T^3 – the appearance of the first transposition of the hexachord in the scene thus coinciding with and drawing attention to one of the crucial dramatic points in the scene: the point at which Wozzeck decides to wade into the pond in search of the murder weapon. Whereas, musically, Part One of the scene was solely concerned with the six-note chord at its original pitch level, Part Two is characterized by its exclusive concern with transposed statements of the chord. Initially, however, Berg is concerned to provide a sense of continuity by using transpositions that are closely linked to the original 'tonic' form or to one another through various common notes. As Ex. 31 illustrates, the new T^3 level of the chord introduced at this point, for example, has three of its six notes in common with the earlier T^0 form.

Ex. 31

The main musical features of the section may be summarized thus:

(1) Beginning on the last quaver of bar 268, the T^3 form of the hexachord (sustained on muted solo violins) overlaps with another version (sustained on muted solo violas) at T^8 – the transposition which has the maximum number of notes (four) in common with T^3.

(2) A version of the 'knife leitmotive', formed from simultaneously ascending and descending chromatic statements of the six-note chord, reaches its goal on a T^5 transposition of the hexachord at bar 274. T^5 is one of the two transpositions which have the maximum number of four notes in common with the original T^0 form. The other of these two 'maximally invariant' transpositions (T^7) will appear in the final section.

(3) The second crucial dramatic moment in the scene, the point at which the tragedy finally becomes inevitable, is the moment at bar 275 when Wozzeck first imagines that he is covered with blood and must wade further into the pond to wash himself clean. Until this point Berg has been careful to use only those transpositions of the hexachord which, because of their common notes, will promote a sense of harmonic continuity. This decisive turning point in the drama, however, is marked by a sudden shift to the most remote possible transposition of the hexachord, the T^6 transposition, which has the fewest possible notes (only one note) in common with the original.

(4) Overlapping statements of the hexachord at various and rapidly changing transpositional levels (bars 276–83) culminate in the 'drowning music' (bars 284–302), in which the hexachord returns to its original spacing but undergoes a series of chromatic ascents, each slower and of narrower compass than the one before. This passage is a vivid representation of events as they are seen through the eyes of Wozzeck himself; a compelling and effective representation of the water rising as, wading further into the pond, he submerges and drowns. The Doctor and the Captain enter and listen as

the chromatic ascents slow down and the surface of the water is still once more.

Part Three: bars 302–91: The Captain and the Doctor leave

The final section of the scene begins at bar 302 as Wozzeck drowns and the chromatic scales finally settle onto a single held chord, the six-note chord at its original pitch level (although an octave lower than on its first appearance) and with its original spacing. This chord is then held as a pedal chord throughout the rest of the scene.

In terms of the way in which the original hexachord is handled, the three sections of the scene as a whole can, therefore, be regarded as defining a formal design similar to that of a traditional ABA structure, the two outer sections (which are exclusively concerned with the T^0 level of the chord) presenting 'tonally' stable areas while the dramatically more tense central section, which avoids the T^0 form in favour of a variety of rapidly changing transpositions, acts as a 'modulating' development section.

It is perhaps coincidental, though nonetheless noteworthy, that the two transpositions most closely related to the original T^0 form of the hexachord are those at T^5 and T^7, that is at the perfect fourth and perfect fifth above (the 'subdominant' and 'dominant' transpositions that in tonal music are the keys most closely related to the tonic); similarly the least closely related transposition of the original hexachord is that at the tritone, T^6, the most remote transposition of a tonic key in tonal music. The toads around the pond begin to croak again at bars 308–14 as the 'toad music' of Part One returns, its superimposed 'abstract' ostinati now enriched by the addition of yet more layers. The original ostinato figure of bars 227–9 now appears a perfect fourth lower than earlier, on the notes C, B, A♯. The notes C and B, which are not components of the six-note chord at its primary pitch level, are derived from a T^7 version of the hexachord which, as is shown in Ex. 32, is here superimposed on the T^0 form. As we have already observed, T^7, along with T^5, is the other maximally invariant transposition of the original hexachord.

Ex. 32

bar 302

Ex. 32 (*cont.*)

The same maximally invariant T^7 form determines the pitch at which the 'moon music' reappears at bar 306, when the Captain comments on the strange atmosphere created by the grey mist and the blood-red moon. The distinctive T^7 elements of the 'toad music', that is to say the notes C and B♮, disappear eight bars before the end of the scene, leaving only the original T^0 elements sustained on the strings and the repeated B♭–D♭ minor third, recalling the opening 'Das Messer', on the timpani.

The Captain urges the Doctor to leave quickly (it is the only time in the opera that the Captain's habitual 'langsam' is replaced by a request that something be done 'schnell') and the two hurry away. As they do so the timpani's B♭–D♭ minor third expands chromatically outwards to A–D and the final D minor orchestral interlude begins.

7 A suggested interpretation

It may seem paradoxical that Berg should set a play dealing with the mental collapse of an individual to music as formalized and as rigorously worked out as the previous chapters have shown that of *Wozzeck* to be. Why choose to depict mental instability through a musical structure that could hardly be more rational?

In his 1929 lecture on *Wozzeck*, which is reprinted in the final part of this book, Berg himself gave only technical reasons for his choice of musical structures, suggesting that, in the absence of tonality, such formal designs were necessary in order to ensure the musical unity of the work, to give a 'sense of self-containedness not only in the small-scale structure of the scenes themselves but also in the larger structure of the single acts and in the architecture of the work as a whole'. We should not take Berg's explanation entirely at face value, however, for, as George Perle has observed, not only is Berg always at his most secretive when he seems to be most open, but he is here (perhaps deliberately) ignoring the implications which the choice of so rigorous a formal design has for the meaning of the opera. It is an explanation that, in fact, ignores just that relation between musical and dramatic structure that plays so important a role in Berg's view of how music drama should operate.

As many of the reviews quoted in the following chapter demonstrate, *Wozzeck* has usually been seen as a work of social protest, an interpretation to which Berg himself lent weight when he pointed out that 'From the moment the curtain parts until it closes for the last time, there is no one in the audience who pays any attention to the various fugues, inventions, suites, sonata movements, variations and passacaglias – no one who heeds anything but the vast social implications of this opera, which by far transcend the personal identity of Wozzeck.'

In both the play and the opera, however, there are other, less obvious, implications that reach beyond an interpretation which

59

regards them only as works of social protest. The Doctor's and the Captain's obsession with time, Wozzeck's hallucinatory visions and the sense of the strangeness and alien-ness of the natural world that permeates the work, all introduce into the play an element of mystery that fits uneasily into any simple socio-economic interpretation. As Victor Price has remarked of the Büchner play, '*Woyzeck* is not a *pièce-à-thèse*. . .it is neither slice-of-life naturalism nor larger-than-life expressionism, nor is it an anti-militaristic tract. . .it is something far more complex than any of these.'[1] It is these other mysterious areas of experience hinted at in the Büchner play that Berg emphasizes through his choice of musical structures and it is through this emphasis that the opera becomes, as we said in the introductory chapter, a protest against both an inhuman and sadistic social order and an uncaring and hostile world.

We have already commented upon the way in which the opera as a whole, with its two more loosely structured outer acts enclosing the tauter symphonic second act, forms what Berg himself called 'a traditional three-part ABA structure', and on the way in which the symmetry of this overall design is underlined by the correspondence between the two most striking visual effects in the opera – the setting of the red sun in Act I scene 2 and the rising of the blood-red moon in Act III scene 2. Berg's love of intricate symmetrical designs, and especially of those that involve large-scale palindromic or retrograde motion, is well known and has already been discussed in Chapter 3. *Wozzeck* contains a host of such symmetries:

> The whole of Act I is framed by two statements of the same theme, the opening oboe melody of Act I scene 1, bars 1–2 which returns in the trombones at the high point of scene 5 (bar 712), immediately before the closing curtain.
>
> Wozzeck's exit in Act I scene 3 (bar 454) is accompanied by an almost literal inversion of the motive which accompanies his entrance earlier in the same scene (bar 427), while the scene as a whole is framed by symmetrically placed statements of the same fanfare-like figure (cf. bars 317–18 and 480–2).
>
> Descending octave transpositions of a figure accompany the rise of the curtain on Act I scene 4; ascending octave transpositions accompany the fall of the curtain as the close of the same scene.
>
> The G–D pedal of the music that introduces Act I scene 5, returns as the curtain falls at the conclusion of the scene.

The harmonic figure that marks the close of Act I also marks the opening of Act II, where it occurs as part of an introductory passage that is itself symmetrical, the notes of the ascending initial arpeggio recurring in reverse order immediately before the rise of the curtain.

The descending 'C major glissando' in the harp which brings down the curtain on the first scene of Act III is mirrored in the ascending 'C major glissando' to which the curtain rises on the second scene.

The central scene of the opera, Act II scene 3, is framed by the two parts of a palindrome, the music which leads into the scene (bars 363–7) returning in retrograde at the end of the scene (bars 406–11), where it leads into the following orchestral interlude.

A particularly mysterious retrograde links the final bars of Act II and the opening bars of Act III. Act II ends with four silent bars, the first two (both marked by pauses) accompanying a motionless stage-picture, the second two defining the precise duration of the closing curtain. Act III commences with a retrograde statement of these four silent bars, which are replaced by two bars of doubled durational value, the first (marked by a pause) again defining the precise duration of the rising curtain (moving at exactly the same pace as the falling curtain that closed the preceding act) and the second accompanying a motionless stage-picture. The two silent stage-pictures are visual and dramatic parallels of each other: at the conclusion of Act II we see Wozzeck seated on his bed in the barracks, staring in front of him, after his trouncing by the Drum Major; the rising curtain of Act III shows us Marie, alone, with her Bible, seated at the table.

The meaning of these symmetries, palindromes and retrogrades is suggested in the very first scene of the opera. The opening words are those of the Captain: 'Langsam, Wozzeck, langsam!' ('Slowly, Wozzeck, slowly'). The words are sung to a melodic figure that, taking the repeated Db in the cor anglais as its starting point, expands to fill chromatically the tritone F–B (Ex. 33). Since, as we have observed in Chapter 6, the tritone F–B is to acquire a particularly fateful significance during the course of the opera, its appearance here, at the very beginning of the work, in association with the word 'langsam' will, in retrospect, imbue this sentence with a simi-

Ex. 33

larly fateful meaning. The concept of time, touched on in the very first words of the opera, is one of the chief subjects of *Wozzeck*. It forms, in different guises, the common obsession of both the Captain and the Doctor. In the case of the Captain the obsession takes the form of a morbid fear of the passing of time, in the case of the Doctor a desire to defeat time through the immortality which he believes that his scientific experiments will bring him. The manic nature of the Doctor's obsession is ironically underlined in Act II scene 2 when his demands that the Captain hurry (bars 184–5: 'Pressiert, pressiert, pressiert!') are set to the motive to which he originally diagnosed Wozzeck's supposed 'aberatio mentalis, second species' in Act I scene 4 (bars 569–72).

Act I scene 1 is dominated by the Captain's discussions on the nature of time. At bars 32–3 the word 'eternity' is symbolized by a fragment of the infinite cycle of perfect fifths. The association of the concept of time and cyclic movement appears in a more overt form later in the scene, however, when the Captain expresses his fear of the passing of time in two powerful verbal images: that of the spherical globe rotating day after day and that of the circular mill-wheel endlessly turning: 'I shudder when I think that the world revolves in a single day, and whenever I see a mill-wheel I feel melancholy'. When, at the end of the scene, the Captain returns to the opening topic of conversation, the textual return is symbolized by a reprise of the music of the opening Prelude. The reprise of this opening music has a deeper symbolic meaning, however, for the music returns not in its original form but in a retrograde version (bars 157–70 corresponding to bars 14–4). Like the endlessly turning mill-wheel, both music and words pursue a circular course and the scene ends as it began.

Retrograde motion in Berg's music always has a particular symbolic or metaphoric significance. T. W. Adorno, a pupil of Berg and someone familiar with the composer's way of thinking, has pointed out that retrogrades and palindromes are 'anti-time' in that they deny time by returning to the point at which they began and thus symbolically erasing what has taken place.[2]

All Berg's mature music, with the exception of the Violin Concerto, includes large-scale palindromes and in those cases where the work has either a text or a programme that is known to us, these palindromes are always associated with the idea of negation. It is significant that, although the assumption that a note-row can be used in its retrograde as easily as in its prime and inverted forms is one of the basic postulates of twelve-note music, distinct retrograde forms play no part in Berg's usual twelve-note practice. In Berg's music the twelve-note set is associated with a specific linear contour which 'in some instances is assumed to retain its identity when it is inverted but never when it is reversed. Thus the retrograde and the retrograde inversion – aspects of the series that are less likely to be melodically identifiable with the prime – are almost never employed.'[3] Since the retrograde forms are not part of Berg's normal twelve-note vocabulary he is thus able to reserve them for specific metaphoric purposes, using them only on occasions when they have the kind of symbolic meaning suggested above and 'as components of a palindrome which embraces the whole music texture'.[4]

The palindromic Film Music interlude at the centre of *Lulu*, for example, marks the turning point of the whole opera, the point at which, after Lulu's ascent through society in the earlier scenes, begins the descent which will lead to the nightmare world of the final scenes of the opera. Elsewhere in *Lulu* small palindromes are similarly used to express negation or denial. When in Act I scene 2 Dr Schoen says to the painter 'I didn't come here to create a scandal, I came to save you from one', the negation of the first by the second half of the sentence is expressed musically by setting the second half as an exact retrograde of the first. When in Act II scene 2 Alwa remarks to Lulu that she can still compare with her portrait, the qualification implicit in her reply ('But my face is thinner') is also expressed by setting her words to a retrograde statement of the music that accompanied Alwa's observation.

Most revealing of the symbolic significance which Berg attached to such retrogrades is the comment that he himself wrote in the annotated score of the third movement of the *Lyric Suite*. The third movement of the *Lyric Suite* depicts the gradual recognition and acknowledgment of the mutual love of Berg and Hanna Fuchs-

Robettin (the woman to whom the work is in reality – and in spite of the dedication which is printed in the published score – dedicated), a recognition symbolized by the *misterioso* scurrying patterns in which the notes representing their respective initials (A, B, H, F – the German names for the notes A, B♭, B and F) are intertwined. Since Berg and Hanna were both married, their love was inevitably doomed from the outset, a fact that is symbolically recognized in the last section of the third movement, in which the music of the opening section is repeated in retrograde, the music returning to the point at which it started. As a verbal acknowledgment of this musical symbol Berg writes in the annotated score, at the point at which the retrograde starts, 'Forget it'.[5]

The association of such retrograde motion with the idea of time here, in the first scene of *Wozzeck*, is therefore of particular significance. In the libretto both the image of the turning globe and the image of the mill-wheel present the idea of time moving in a circle. Similarly in the music the retrograde movement, once started, runs its predetermined course to return, like the turning earth and mill-wheel, to the point at which it started. At two points in the opera Wozzeck's impending mental collapse is specifically associated with palindromic figurations: in Act I scene 3, when Marie, voicing her fears of such a collapse, remarks 'He'll drive himself crazy with those ideas of his' (bars 459–60), and in Act II scene 3 (bars 400–2), when Wozzeck, horrified by the implications of Marie's 'Rather a knife in my breast than dare to lay a hand on me', says 'Man is an abyss. You get dizzy looking down into him – I feel dizzy.' That Wozzeck's mental instability is related to his terror of the baleful natural world which he inhabits is suggested in the course of the scene with the Doctor (Act I scene 4) where similarly palindromic figurations appear in a different context. 'Lines, circles, strange figures – if only one could read them', says Wozzeck as he tries to describe to the Doctor his feelings that the toadstool rings in the field hide mysterious messages within them. Written as a single 7/4 bar, the music itself describes a circular figure as the voice part, outlining a descending whole-tone scale and its retrograde, is accompanied at the same time by its inversion and diminution in the orchestra (Ex. 34).

Although Wozzeck confesses himself unable to decipher the message which he believes the 'lines, circles and strange figures' to conceal,

Ex. 34

he instinctively feels a terror of the predestined course of events which the musical palindromes reveal to be the meaning of the toad-stool rings.

We have said earlier that the musical forms chosen for some of the scenes in *Wozzeck* (the baroque suite of Act I scene 1 or the pas-sacaglia of Act I scene 4 for example) symbolize the psychological or dramatic kernel of the scene. But, in fact, every aspect of the highly formalized structure of the opera – from the large-scale design to small details of the kind discussed in the preceding para-graph – has symbolic significance. The rigorously determined struc-ture of the work, with its autonomous self-contained formal designs, symbolizes not the mental disintegration of the chief protagonist but that mechanistic and uncaring universe within which he finds himself trapped; the formal design is itself a symbol of that universal inhumanity which leads, as much as do the social conditions and the inhumanity of his fellow men, to Wozzeck's mental collapse. It is a large-scale musico-dramatic symbol that finds its most succinct and poignant form in Act III scene 4, when the sound of the toads returns in the few bars following the death of Wozzeck, their croak-ing represented by a series of mathematically precise, interlocking ostinati. It is a fitting image of a 'fundamentally hostile and inhu-man' universe that continues on its autonomous predetermined course unaffected by the human tragedy that it has just witnessed.

The musical palindromes thus stand as a symbol of predestination and of man's inability to affect the course of events. Like the circular images in the text, the palindromes, returning to the point at which they began, closing the circle and thus symbolically negating their own existence, represent the eventual and inevitable end of these predetermined events. When the constant quaver movement of the final scene is abruptly cut off at the end of the opera there is no feeling of closure or completion. The music, it seems, could continue – indeed, as Berg himself remarked, it *does* continue. The circle is closed and the cycle starts afresh. Nothing has changed. The death of Wozzeck has passed unnoticed, the world continues unaffected and, it is implied, the tragedy is about to be re-enacted with Wozzeck's child.

It is only in the two operas that Berg's obsessive preoccupation with labyrinthine formal designs, intricate symmetries, palindromes, retrogrades and other such 'abstract' and highly organized structural devices is linked to texts which enable us to see something of the private significance which such things had for the composer.

'There is a bit of me in this character', wrote Berg to his wife Helene in 1918, while working on *Wozzeck*.[6] Like so many of Berg's apparently casual comments it is a remark that is more revealing and more accurate than one might at first suppose.

We know that Berg saw in the play and in the situation of its main character things which reminded him of his own spell of service in the Austrian army ('I have been spending these years just as dependent on people that I hate, have been in chains, sick, captive, resigned, in fact humiliated', he wrote in the same letter to his wife) and that he deliberately changed some details of Büchner's text to make them correspond to his own experiences of military service. When Büchner's Doctor instructs Woyzeck 'Erbsen essen, dann Hammelfleisch essen', the Doctor in Berg's opera says 'Bohnen essen, dann Schöpsenfleisch essen', thus turning the sentence into a reference to the meals of beans and mutton ('prepared', according to Berg, 'in the most disgusting manner') that were regularly served to the composer and his fellow soldiers during their period of army training at Bruck.[7] We know from the description that Berg gave in a letter to his pupil Gottfried Kassowitz in 1915 that the army doctor at Bruck reminded him of the inhuman doctor in Büchner's play and that the sound of the sleeping soldiers in his own barracks provided him with the inspiration for the wordless chorus of sleeping soldiers that opens Act II scene 5 of the opera.[8]

Recent revelations also suggest that Berg may have recognized a deeper similarity between his own situation and that of Wozzeck. As a young man Berg had had a love affair as a result of which he became, at the age of seventeen, the father of an illegitimate child, a daughter born on 4 December 1902 and subsequently named Albine. The mother of Berg's daughter was a girl called Marie Scheuchl who worked in the kitchen of the Berghof, the family's summer home in Carinthia. Berg could hardly have failed to see the similarity between himself, the father of an illegitimate child by Marie Scheuchl, and Wozzeck, also the father of an illegitimate child by a woman called Marie. The fact that he sent his daughter Albine a ticket for the first Vienna performance of *Wozzeck* seems to underline the composer's recognition of the relationship between himself and his operatic 'hero'.[9]

But perhaps Berg also saw in *Wozzeck* another reflection of his own personal concerns and obsessions. Like Wozzeck, Berg was predisposed to regard everyday things as having mysterious messages and portents hidden within them. An ardent believer in numerology, he regarded the number 23 as having a peculiar significance for him and was able to discover manifestations of this fateful number in the most unlikely places. So great was his belief in the power of this and other significant numbers that he incorporated them into his music, using them as a means of determining the proportions and the metronome markings of many of his works. He even allowed such numbers to govern the way in which he organized his everday life, arranging to write important letters or to start or finish work on a composition on the 23rd of the month.

Berg himself seems to have regarded his numerological interest as being in some way associated with the passage of time and with predestination, an association that found confirmation in the works of Wilhelm Fliess, with whose pseudo-scientific writings Berg became acquainted in the summer of 1914. Fliess, wrote Berg to Schoenberg in June 1914, had shown that 'life and all phases in the life of all living creatures run in periods and give rise to cycles which are always divisible by 28 and 23, and had demonstrated scientifically that such cycles, governed by laws as strict as those of planetary motion, apply to the dates of birth and death, periods of life, stages in the illness of whole families, generations and even states'.[10] Given such a belief in what Fliess himself called 'a mechanism that informs our hour of birth with the same certainty as that of our death',[11] it is not, perhaps, surprising that Berg recognized in the play's concern with time a subject that reflected his own personal concerns, or that he should choose, through the musical structures and conceits employed in the opera, to suggest his own interpretation of the meaning of the mysterious message concealed in Büchner's toadstool rings.

The inhuman mechanistic universe depicted in *Wozzeck* represents Berg's own view of the universe, a natural world governed by uncaring, mechanical, predetermined processes which operate irrespective of the fate or feelings of the individual. Like Wozzeck, Berg himself found nature terrifying in its intensity and saw in it a symbol of loss of personal identity: 'Some people are so overwhelmed by music', wrote Berg to Helene Berg in 1910, 'that they almost faint when they hear an E minor chord on the piano. I am like that with nature. Even as a small boy, when I was out in the country and the surroundings were too beautiful I just couldn't bear it. . .This fear of nature still clings to me, the knowledge that great beauty in the natural scene drives me into restlessness and dissatisfaction. . . I shun these frightening ecstasies. . .I escape into my room, to my books and scores. I feel that here I am in my own element, my own realm; anywhere else I might fall ill and in nature I should disintegrate and be submerged.'[12]

If the many autobiographical elements which appear in all Berg's music from *Wozzeck* onwards are seen not as signs of the composer's own egotism but as his attempts to capture and assert the value of individual identity and experience, then the structure of *Wozzeck* should be seen as a symbol of the forces in the face of which these attempts are made; an assertion of the nothingness which, despite the Doctor's vain hopes of immortality, is the ultimate end of the transient individual human being in the face of the fatefully and endlessly revolving world that so terrifies the Captain in the opening scene of the opera.

8 Stage history: the premiere and subsequent performances

Conducted by Kleiber, directed by Franz Ludwig Hörth, and designed by Panos Aravantinos, *Wozzeck* finally received its premiere at the State Opera in Berlin on 14 December 1925. The cast included Leo Schützendorf as Wozzeck, Sigrid Johanson as Marie, Waldemar Henke as the Captain, Martin Abendroth as the Doctor, Fritz Soot as the Drum Major and Gerhard Witting as Andres.

Those sections of the press that were opposed to Kleiber continued to campaign against the opera in their reports on the premiere and subsequent performances. The *Berliner Lokalanzeiger*, which had earlier reported that the dress rehearsal of the work had led to riots at the State Opera, falsely claimed that a later performance had to be abandoned because of a demonstration. Paul Zschorlich, the critic of the *Deutsche Zeitung*, devoted his column to a series of attacks on the work, the first of which, on the day following the premiere, reported how

After the second act a small group sought to gain success by force and there were the usual scandalous scenes, which are now inseparable from those premieres at the State Opera that are directed by Mr Kleiber. Violent hisses also ran around the house and there was some whistling. . .After the last act the composer, relying on the instincts of the masses, showed himself holding the hand of the small child who had taken part. It was a touching sight![1]

Describing the opera as a 'frontal attack by atonality on the time-honoured musical fortress of Unter den Linden', Zschorlich observed that:

The music of Alban Berg is truly frightful. Of the harmonic system built up over centuries not one stone is left on top of another. The nastiness and lack of justification of the polyphony breaks even Schoenberg's own world record. Who asks about melody, about emotion, about expression, forms, laws makes himself laughable. . .the work is a catastrophe in our musical development.[2]

The reviews in those papers not politically or artistically biased

69

make it clear, however, that both the public and the majority of critics recognized that *Wozzeck* was a milestone in the history of opera.

To Oskar Bie, writing in the *Berliner Börsencourier* on 15 December, the work was 'assured and controlled; this is no experiment but masterly of its kind, seriously considered and convincingly worked out. The skill of the score is extraordinary.' 'This poor soldier Wozzeck', observed Bie, 'has a double mission in the history of art. In literature he began the new naturalism which Büchner anticipated and Hauptmann realised, and he now also starts the new musical naturalism which Schoenberg introduced in his monodramas and which his pupil Alban Berg has carried over into opera.'[3]

'The evening was not only the greatest success of the season', wrote H. H. Stuckenschmidt in the *Thüringer Allgemeine Zeitung*, 'but a significant event in the history of music drama. In spite of a few die-hards, who had already rudely abused the hospitality of the theatre in the dress rehearsal, the public was overwhelmed by the work.'[4]

In contrast to the 'violent hissing and whistling' described by Zschorlich, the influential Viennese critic Paul Stefan observed in *Die Stunde* that 'a solo whistler remained isolated and his bungling manipulations of a house key raised only laughter in the theatre. . . Alban Berg's opera is by all indications the sensation of the Berlin State Opera; notwithstanding the fact that the battle troops for and against had been brought in the success was enormous.'[5]

In the *Berliner Zeitung am Mittag* Adolf Weissman, having related the countless rumours that had circulated before the first performance, declared that the premiere was 'an artistic achievement of the highest order.'[6]

A less enthusiastic review by Wiegmund Pisling of the *8 Uhr Abendblatt*, in which he confessed himself disconcerted by the structural novelty of the work, is worth quoting at some length since it is amongst the first to raise what was to be a constant topic of discussion in many of the earliest reviews of the opera, the audibility and relevance of the abstract musical forms employed in the piece:

The work is the apotheosis of the 'interesting', of which one can scarcely imagine anything bolder. The attempt to achieve a union of dramatic psychology and the forms of absolute music is interesting enough. But it is certainly no more than that. Let us be satisfied with a single example. The first scene of Act Three (in Marie's room) is built of the following: a theme, six variations and a fugue. We have gone in search of them, have ferreted out these ingenious contrapuntal forms in Universal Edition's beautifully clear piano score. What skill! But these things don't count for much in opera. They are unimportant. They are employed as experiments. Dramatic composition from Monteverdi to Schoenberg's *Erwartung* follows other laws. The canon in *Fidelio* is not beautiful because it is a canon but because it contains beautiful music. And that Pizarro's aria is in a rudimentary sonata form is again of no consequence next to the intensity of the dramatic force. The words with which the Captain judges Wozzeck are also applicable to Berg's intellectualisations: 'He thinks too much; that hurts.'[7]

Addressing himself to the same problem in his *Zeitung am Mittag* review Weissman arrived at different conclusions:

The ordinary listener is not required to admire those moments of this music which are so astonishingly ingenious on paper: he doesn't see them, he hears them. And he must also hear how naturalistic is the handling – how the air quivers, how the spirit trembles. . .in short how the tragedy of the figure of Wozzeck, of Wozzeck's fate, becomes gripping music. Let us not deceive ourselves: the atonality of the music of this *Wozzeck* overpowers us; it is, I believe, the last beam of the light from the spirit of *Tristan* passed through Schoenberg.

Despite the critical and public success, the extended press campaign which preceded and followed the Berlin premiere, and which, amongst other things, suggested that the opera had required 137 rehearsals, left its mark. For many years *Wozzeck* was rumoured to be 'unperformable' and was to attract political controversy.

Amongst the audience at the Berlin premiere had been Otokar Ostrčil, the conductor of the Czech National Opera in Prague. Ostrčil had already expressed interest in the piece, and his determination to perform it was strengthened by the impression which the Berlin production made on him. 'It is a beautiful and powerful work', he wrote a few days after the premiere, 'the most notable foreign opera since Strauss's *Elektra*. The music, in a line from Mahler to Schoenberg, is highly modern, authentic, no *Modenpétarde à la Stravinsky* but something really new, individual and original in expression and structure.'[8] The work was programmed for the following season and, conducted by Ostrčil, received its Prague premiere on 11 November, 1926. The first two performances in Prague were greeted with public and critical acclaim, but by the third performance the opera had again become the target of political protest, in this case by Czech nationalists who objected to a German work being performed at the National Opera rather than at the Deutsches Theater; they wanted

Ostrčil 'to put on the *Bartered Bride* seven evenings a week', commented Berg wryly in a letter to Kleiber.[9] The third Prague performance was stopped before the final act, the theatre cleared and a ban on future performances imposed by the police.

In June 1927 Berg undertook the four-day train journey from Austria to Russia to be present at the Leningrad production of *Wozzeck*, informing his wife in a constant stream of letters and telegrams how the 'very effective' production received 'terrific applause' after the public dress rehearsal on 12 June and was a 'tumultuous success' on the following first night. Reviewing the production in the Leningrad papers the critic Igor Glebov spoke of the way in which:

the persuasive power, the depth and the expression of the music grows from scene to scene and from act to act. The scenes in the tavern and in the barracks at the end of the second act and the whole of the third act cannot fail to seize hold of the listener through the truth and the seriousness of their expression. Here the impartial listener is completely indifferent to the means through which the composer obtains his colossal effects. The music lives and breathes, it communicates the experience and the emotion. . .In this respect I know of no other contemporary opera which has a clearer and more rational basis. The composer seems to have bound himself hand and foot. Wagner is like a lark flying free in the air by comparison. But, in all, there is no more passionate, no more emotionally true or more deeply expressive music drama than this *Wozzeck*.[10]

The critic Vladimir Dranschikov observed that 'the music of *Wozzeck* so grows out of the drama and so accords with human perception that the unprepared and naive listener immediately succumbs to the magic of its voice, even though in this opera the singing voice, at the frontiers of intensity, often gives way to spoken melody'.[11]

In the ten years following the Russian revolution Leningrad had established itself as a particularly active centre of contemporary art. The reviews quoted above reflect the interest and the enthusiasm of the many devotees of 'new music' at the time. It was an enthusiasm that was allowed to flourish for only a short time. Within six months the official political attitude to such 'advanced' music was beginning to change, and *Wozzeck* was dropped from the programme of the forthcoming 1927–28 season. The opera that the Nazis were later to ban as an example of 'cultural bolshevism' was regarded by the Soviet authorities as an example of 'decadent bourgeois art'. At time of writing *Wozzeck* has still not been revived in the USSR.

News of the Prague debacle soon spread to Vienna and, although the scandal had had little to do with Berg's opera, cast a shadow over the future of *Wozzeck* that the successful Leningrad production could not dispel. Only another successful German production could rehabilitate the work. Berg was, therefore, particularly anxious that the fourth production of *Wozzeck* under Johannes Schüler in Oldenburg in March 1929 should be a success; he adapted the score to suit the reduced orchestral forces available in Oldenburg and, for the first time, delivered a lecture on the work before the performance.[12] The following letter, written on Christmas Eve 1928 to the head of Universal Edition's opera department, shows the extent to which he showered Schüler and the Oldenburg production team with advice and suggestions and the extent to which Berg involved himself generally in subsequent provincial productions of the work:

Dear Dr Heinsheimer,

I should like to ask you to tell the gentlemen who reported to you the plans for doing *Wozzeck* at Oldenburg how very happy I am about this piece of good news and how I am full of the most pleasant expectations for Feb. 21.

I should also like to use this opportunity to ask you to inform them of the following wishes, suggested to me by my experiences with the State Theatres in Berlin, Prague and Leningrad, concerning the performance.

(1) Pay particular attention to studying the stage music, possibly reinforcing the violin and guitar (by 2, 3 or even 4 parts) and also the accordion if this is necessary on dynamic grounds. As much like chamber music as possible, especially the 'Preacher' (Schoenberg's *Pierrot* may be regarded as a model!). N.B. Please don't exaggerate the tone of this sermon: it should not be done with an excess of drunkenness but throughout there should run more of a feeling of bonhomie.

(2) I am quite prepared to undertake revisions in the vocal parts if it is worth it for the benefit of other, often more important, artistic considerations; if, for example, a particularly suitable interpreter of a role was unable to do it because of a few low (or high) notes. This, of course, must be done by myself. If such revisions are found necessary they can indicate the passage to me.

(3) The first trombone which is designated 'alto trombone' in the score should not be one of those quite small instruments which are used in jazz bands nowadays but an instrument which is on a level with the other trombones. As a matter of fact up to now it has been played throughout by the first tenor trombone and has been transposed into the tenor where written in the alto.

(4) I attach great importance to the lack of any pause between the separate scenes. Restrict the sets to the absolute minimum rather than make the orchestra wait for a change. This applies particularly to the third scene of the last act which can scarcely be indicated in too insubstantial a way. It would then be possible to have a very quick change for the fourth scene.

(5) Great value is placed on the realism of the whole mise-en-scène; above all in the 'nature scenes' (I/2, III/2 and III/5).

(6) I am, of course, very willing to advise or otherwise be of service to the Landestheater on the basis of my previous experience of productions of *Wozzeck*.

Those, dear Dr Heinsheimer, are all the fairly important things that occur to me at the moment. I once more beg you to give the gentlemen in Oldenburg my friendliest greetings and to wish them the best for their production.

The triumphant Oldenburg *Wozzeck* had its premiere on 5 March 1929. 'The applause grew after every act', wrote Dr Konrad Bartosch in the Oldenburg *Stadt und Land*, 'and at the end reached an ovation for the Landestheater, for all the cast and for the composer, who was present – an ovation such as we have not experienced in the eight opera seasons since the war. The composer, director, conductor and soloists were called out innumerable times.'[13] 'All in all, an event even for the hard-boiled critic,' wrote T. W. Werner in the *Hannover Kurier*, while the Oldenburg *Volksblatt* called the production 'a success such as has rarely appeared in the history of the Oldenburg Landestheater – a success without precedent. . .not only because of the triumph of Alban Berg's music but also because of the gigantic achievement of the Oldenburg Landesorchester and the Oldenburg Opera.'[14] Manfred Bukofzer, writing in the Dortmund *General-Anzeiger*, was not slow to point out the implication of the Oldenburg achievement: 'The work which until now only Berlin, Prague, and Leningrad have risked, which because of its difficulties and demands has again been removed from the prospectus of the Vienna State Opera, has now been produced on the provincial stage of Oldenburg.'[15]

What the conductor Johannes Schüler was later to call the 'fairytale of the insurmountable difficulty of the opera' had been disproved. Before the Berlin premiere the press had claimed that the work had required an unprecedented 137 rehearsals; Oldenburg had now shown that a small, provincial opera house could mount this 'unplayable' work with 32 rehearsals. Replying to a letter of congratulations from Universal Edition, Schüler wrote, 'Your pleasure wholly matches that of the director, of myself, and of all my colleagues. If a general success comes as a result of this local success, if the ban is broken on this unsurpassed work (to my mind a work that cannot be excelled in form and musical thought), the path of which has been sadly obstructed – then the last and the real goal of our efforts has been achieved.'[16] As Josef Lex, who sang the role of Wozzeck in Oldenburg, observed, the success of the production 'broke like a hurricane and signified the final victory of the work'.[17]

As a result of the Oldenburg production many small companies became interested in the work, and in the twelve months from December 1929 to December 1930 seven provincial opera houses staged productions of *Wozzeck* – Essen (December 1929), Aachen (February 1930), Düsseldorf (April 1930), Königsberg (May 1930), Lübeck (May 1930), Cologne (October 1930), and Gera (December 1930). Anxious to ensure the continued success of the opera, Berg attended most of these performances and repeated the introductory lecture that he had prepared for Oldenburg.

Not all of these seven productions were equally successful. The Aachen production, which Heinrich Jalowetz was later to describe as the 'best stage production I have ever heard',[18] and which Berg himself thought 'excellent' and regarded as a model, was an unqualified success. This production was taken on tour and performed in Liège, Amsterdam, and Rotterdam in the course of the 1930–31 season and played an important role in making the opera known. The Gera production was also greeted with acclaim, the critics referring to the 'innumerable curtain calls which were the public's thanks for the immeasurable efforts of all those concerned' and describing the opera itself as 'extraordinarily successful. . .a work of astounding proportions and deep psychology'.[19] In Königsberg, which a local reviewer described as 'being considered, not without justice, a conservative town,' the work was, according to the critic of the *Ostpreussische Zeitung,* a 'decided flop'. 'Our public', wrote the critic, 'by its icy reserve rejected the work. It was right to do so. One cannot ask a listener trained in the classics to accept a music the first premise of which is the denial of all established tradition.'[20]

The provincial premiere which caused Berg the most worry, however, was that at Essen in December 1929, the first of the productions after that in Oldenburg. The main cause of Berg's worries were the sets by Caspar Neher, the designer for the first performances of many of the works of Kurt Weill and Bertolt Brecht. In this Essen production, wrote Berg to Schoenberg on 10 December 1929, *Wozzeck* would be 'nothing but a "Twopenny Opera" by C. Neher, after Büchner by Berg'.[21] On the following day Berg wrote to his publishers that the sets were 'so insane' that they were likely 'seriously to endanger the success of the work.' 'Of course', wrote Berg, 'I have tried to soften things where I can (by getting rid of the urinal that I forgot to compose into the inn-scene, for example), to put back the many things I can remember which Neher has tried to conceal and to save some of the production.'[22] Yet even three days before the opening night Berg was still forced to confess to Webern that he was 'terrified for the Essen premiere'.[23] In the event, the production was moderately successful and the critics seem to have admired the sets which so worried the composer. A generally unfavourable review in the Essen *Volkszeitung* suggested that 'the sets of Caspar Neher interpreted the dark, melancholy content of Büchner's work better than did the music' and went on to comment that 'the full house appreciated the achievements of our artists but the impression of the work itself remains in dispute. . .It may be doubted whether it was necessary for our opera management to burden our theatre with this production. . .It is regrettable that a repertory piece should have been put off because of this *Wozzeck*.'[24] A more favourably disposed critic, however, interpreted the lack of acclaim by the people of Essen as being itself an indication of the power of the work: '*Wozzeck* does not belong amongst those operas that have a noisy "success" – certainly in this sense the West German premiere was a success and the artists had to appear many times in front of the curtain. The true success, in comparison, remains unseen because it presupposes a violent emotion, an emotion which must prevent all loud applause. But such an emotion was, without doubt, present at the Essen premiere and thus the work had a double success.'[25]

On 30 March 1930 *Wozzeck* was finally produced at the State Opera in Vienna. During the rehearsal period in Vienna, as in Berlin, various stories began to circulate about the 'impossible' difficulties which the opera was supposed to present. The work was again said to be 'unplayable,' of 'Babylonian complexity,' and it was rumoured that the Vienna Philharmonic was having to be rehearsed section by section – a thing that had never happened before. A joke current at the time told of how a member of the orchestra, when asked by an acquaintance how things were going, was said to have replied, 'With luck we'll be over the hill [Berg].'[26] More serious, and more ominous in view of future events, was the extent to which the opera again became the focus of political disagreements. On 29 March 1930, the day before the Vienna premiere, the *Deutscheöster-reichische Tageszeitung*, the official paper of the Austrian National Socialist Party, wrote:

One of the most provocative agit-prop pieces [*Tendenzstücke*] ever writ-ten, Alban Berg's opera *Wozzeck*, after Georg Büchner, receives its first performance at the Vienna State Opera on Sunday. The work was a failure in Berlin and Prague and only kept its place in the Berlin repertory as a result of the contract with the Viennese publishers Universal Edition, who, as is well known, publish all the works of the Schoenberg circle and are gener-

ally responsible for the whole of the Jewish radical Schoenberg hotch-
potch. Only in Leningrad did *Wozzeck* meet with any approval. The Social
Democrats, along with the rowdy Universal Edition and Schoenberg circle,
will do everything possible on Sunday to make propaganda for this un-
speakable, botched work with which our opera will be disgraced. The sound
sense of the Viennese public will give these compromising Austro-Marxist
activities of the management of the State Theatre the answer they deserve.[27]

As Webern reported in a letter to Schoenberg, the success of the
Vienna premiere was 'really quite tremendous' and Berg had to take
thirteen curtain calls. Webern, who was seeing the opera for the first
time, confessed that it had 'shaken him to the depths'.[28]

Berg said that he had never before heard the piece performed so
perfectly and declared himself overwhelmed by the 'love with which
all involved had embraced his concerns'.[29] The press reviews were
generally favourable, although many of the critics of the right-wing
papers abhorred the piece. Hans Liebstöckl, of the *Sonn- und
Montagszeitung* described the opera as 'hateful' and ascribed its success to the efforts of 'a particularly hardworking claque': 'One can
hardly suppose,' wrote Liebstöckl, 'that the music itself, without
melody or line, really found so many enthusiastic supporters.'[30]
Julius Korngold, the influential critic of the *Neue Freie Presse*, saw
the piece as a third-rate proletarian *Pelléas* and declared that 'if this
is the music of the future then it has nothing to offer'. The anonymous critic of the *Deutscheösterreichische Tageszeitung* described
the melodic invention as being 'on the whole, exceptionally poor and
hopelessly primitive:

Dissonances are, of course, the norm. The handling of the voices is frankly
repellent; they groan, cry, squeak, yodel, howl, and do everything but sing. If
such things spread then all singing teachers can quietly pack their bags: one
will not be able to talk of 'singing' any more.[31]

The year 1931 saw the staging of a further eight productions of
Wozzeck, six of them by provincial German opera houses (at
Braunschweig, Darmstadt, Frankfurt, Wuppertal, Freiburg, and
Leipzig) and one at the State Theatre in Zurich. The most significant
of the 1931 productions, however, was that given in Philadelphia,
where *Wozzeck* received its American premiere under Leopold
Stokowski on 19 March. So great was the interest in the premiere,
according to *The New York Evening Post*, that 'a special train
conveyed across three state lines more of the Manhattan curious than
can be counted upon to patronize some relatively important events at
home.' The premiere was greeted as being 'the most significant event

of New York's waning music season' and the work was described as 'a masterpiece of opera such as has not come from the Old World to the New since *Pelléas et Mélisande* and *Boris Godunoff*'.[32] In November 1931 the Philadelphia Opera Company brought *Wozzeck* to New York City for the first time. Amongst the audience on that occasion was Louis Krasner, the young violinist who was later to commission Berg to write the Violin Concerto.

February 1932 saw the Belgian premiere at the Théâtre de la Monnaie in Brussels. According to the *Revue Musicale* the soloists had been studying the opera since the previous May and it was said that there had been 229 solo and 44 orchestral and ensemble rehearsals. Despite this intense preparation, however, Berg, who travelled to Brussels for the premiere, was worried about the work's chances of success. 'It's possible that we shan't even have the usual *Wozzeck* success', he wrote to Helene. 'The audiences here are very conservative.'[33] Berg was also worried about the conductor Corneil de Thoran, who, Berg reported, had 'studied the work down to the last detail' but whose performance left a lot to be desired: 'He looks so superb you'd think he feels all the subtlety and warmth and bloom of the music and could convey it. But it's mostly stiff semiquavers.'[34] Despite Berg's worries the Belgian premiere was, as he telegraphed Helene, a 'very great success': 'Packed house in excited mood from the start – four curtains after the first act, six after the second and at the end, when I appeared, a great ovation from the whole audience.' The conservative Belgian press was less enthusiastic about the work, the *Etoile Belge* describing the piece as 'a victim of its own system': 'the atonal opera of Alban Berg becomes a prisoner of its methods, a slave of its form so that what it wins in formal strength it sacrifices in invention and expression'.[35]

By this time, however, the political troubles which had affected *Wozzeck* throughout its early career were becoming an ever more serious factor in its fortunes. The growing influence of the Nazis was beginning to affect the willingness of theatre managers to stage so radical an opera. With the exception of a new staging at the Berlin State Opera there were only two German productions of *Wozzeck* in 1932, and a number of houses (such as Coburg and Mainz) that had planned to stage the piece gave in to political pressure at the last moment. As early as 1930 the critic of the Viennese newspaper *Signale* had protested that 'One can hardly say anything after the first performance about the success of this novelty. Berg and his *Wozzeck* have become the concern of musical and political party loyalties to such an extent that approval and opposition are not spontaneous but engineered. One must wait. With luck one will not have to wait until 1950.'[36] Events were to prove the *Signale* critic a realist. The new staging of *Wozzeck* which Erich Kleiber, with characteristic bravery, mounted in Berlin on 30 November 1932 was to be the last production of the opera on a German stage for sixteen years. The production which opened in Brno in December 1932 was the last production before the Nazis came to power in January 1933.

On 30 November 1934 Kleiber conducted the premiere of the 'Symphonic Pieces' from Berg's new opera *Lulu* in Berlin and, four days later, resigned his post at the Staatsoper. On 7 December, three days after Kleiber's resignation, Goebbels made a speech in the Berlin Sportplatz in which he denounced the 'moral decay of the atonal composers', declaring that atonality 'furnished the most dramatic proof of how strongly the Jewish intellectual infection had taken hold of the national body'. The immediate target of the attack was Hindemith, whom Furtwängler had publicly defended, but the wider implications of the speech were made clear in the following January edition of *Die Musik* which, commenting on the press reception of the *Lulu* Pieces, said:

The accounts of the performance of Alban Berg's symphonic suite from his opera *Lulu* demonstrates the ideological confusion and the lack of aesthetic understanding of the majority of Berlin's critics. It is significant that one of the most degraded foreign yellow newspapers, the *Neues Wiener Journal*, was able to quote several Berlin reviews which seemed favourably inclined towards the emigré musical Jews. . .such reviews are inadmissable in our age of directed public opinion, for they befuddle the mind and hinder the rebuilding of our culture. The National Association of the German Press would do well to reexamine basically the fitness of these reviewers for their job.[37]

Even before Berg had officially become a proscribed composer, however, his music had, with the single exception of Kleiber's performance of the *Lulu* Pieces, disappeared from the stages and concert halls of Germany. At the same time the most powerful orchestral and operatic managements in Vienna, mindful of the situation across the border and of the growing Austrian support for the Nazis, became more and more unwilling to programme Berg's compositions. Berg, who depended upon the royalties from the performances of *Wozzeck* ('I benefit a hundred times more from a single 'disputed' opera performance than from the success of the *Lyric Suite* in twenty big towns', he had written to Kleiber in July 1931), was financially and artistically ruined by the disappearance of the opera from the concert halls of Germany, Austria and eventually Europe.

Berg heard *Wozzeck* once more before his death in December 1935, when a concert performance on 14 March 1935 from the Queen's Hall in London under Adrian Boult, with Richard Bitterauf (the Aachen Wozzeck) in the title role, was broadcast by the BBC and transmitted into Austria by Swiss Radio. 'I want to take the opportunity of saying how deeply happy the BBC *Wozzeck* has made me', wrote Berg to Edward Clark on 22 March, 'To my admiration for the BBC is now added that for the marvellous Mr Boult'[38] Berg's pupil Heinrich Jalowetz, who had conducted the first Viennese performance of the *Three Fragments from 'Wozzeck'* in 1926, later wrote to the composer describing the Boult performance as 'an exceptional experience'. 'I have never had so overpowering an impression', wrote Jalowetz, '. . .in spite of the lack of scenery and action the work made so strong and completely unexpected an impression. It was the most eloquent testimony to this music and to those who performed it. And it means – and this is the happiest part of the evening – that music, and particularly your music, is still, in spite of everything, a universal language and that to perform good music well one need be neither "indigenous" nor an "initiate" but only a good musician.'[39]

It had already been suggested to Berg that a successful performance at the Queen's Hall might lead to a staging of the work at Covent Garden. By January 1935 plans for this production were well under way and the producer Otto Erhardt had spent some time in Vienna discussing the work with the composer. 'I am looking forward to the Covent Garden *Wozzeck*', wrote Berg to Schoenberg on 30 January, 'and have just been through the whole production with the producer here in Vienna. I hope that I shall be invited – if only to get away from this artistically unfriendly atmosphere for once.' In the event the plan came to nothing. Covent Garden had hoped to buy the costumes and scenery for the production from German and Austrian opera houses that had staged the work; by 1935, however, Nazi pressure had led these houses to destroy the *Wozzeck* scenery and they were unable to help.[40]

Between the BBC performance in London in 1934 and the first post-war performance fourteen years later, there was only a single production of *Wozzeck*, at the Teatro Reale dell'Opera in Rome in November 1942, where the work was included, despite German objections, in a short season of contemporary operas performed under Tullio Serafin. Tito Gobbi sang the title role.

Although the first post-war *Wozzeck* was a staged production in Düsseldorlf in June 1948, many of the immediate post-war performances of *Wozzeck* – in London in April 1949, in Paris in December 1950 and in New York in April 1951 – were, like that in London in 1934, concert performances. The rehabilitation of the opera as a stage work, and its gradual acceptance as a piece that could take its place in the repertoire, began with two productions (at the Teatro San Carlo in Naples in December 1950 and in the Salzburger Festspielhaus on 16 August 1951) conducted by Karl Böhm, who was to become closely associated with the opera, and the British premiere at the Royal Opera House Covent Garden in January 1952.

To post-war critics, who had become familiar with the opera only in the concert hall and through broadcasts, the dramatic impact of the work in the theatre was overwhelming. Writing in *Opera* magazine about the effect of the Neapolitan production, Harold Rosenthal observed:

Concert performances and broadcasts from the continent had in some way prepared one for the impact of this work but it is not until one has the opportunity of seeing it in the theatre than one can appreciate the full measure of its power and drama. In more than 15 years of opera-going I have never spent such an absorbing evening in an opera house nor have I ever emerged feeling so completely shattered emotionally and physically. . .of the many duties that the Covent Garden Opera Trust has to fulfil to the opera public an early production of *Wozzeck* is one of the most important.[41]

When Covent Garden mounted its production in 1952 the British press, recognizing the importance of the event, rose to the occasion. A special preview issue of *Opera* the month before the premiere included an introductory article on the opera by Erwin Stein, an article on Büchner by Hugo Garten and a translation of Berg's own article 'The musical forms in my opera "Wozzeck"'. *The Musical Times* sent a team of five critics to review the production, most of whom reacted in the same way as Rosenthal to seeing the opera on stage. Arthur Jacobs, who had attended both the 1949 London performance and the 1951 concert performance under Dimitri Mitropolous in New York, admitted to approaching the stage presentation with some misgivings:

No doubt it was unwise to come to *Wozzeck* with as high an expectation as I had. So often one is disappointed when looking forward not merely to hearing a performance but to re-living or intensifying an experience. . .I was not disappointed. . .Even those parts of the score most striking in themselves seem to gain by their theatrical setting. Take, for instance, the stupendous crescendo for the whole orchestra on the single note B (after the death of Marie) building up a tension which suddenly collapses as the out-of-tune piano starts the wild polka on a distorted chord of C major. How much is added by the fact that the crescendo takes place in the darkened theatre, with the curtain down and that the piano's entry coincides with the raising of the curtain on the populated interior of a shabbily-lit tavern!. . .nothing marred my impression that I was undergoing one of the major operatic experiences of my life.[42]

William Mann similarly declared that 'people, like me. . .who had not seen *Wozzeck* in the theatre before will remember that per-formance as one of the great operatic experiences of their lives'.

The cast of the first Covent Garden production on 22 January 1952 included Marko Rothmüller as Wozzeck, Christel Goltz as Marie, Parry Jones as the Captain, Fredrick Dalberg as the Doctor and Thorensteinn Hannesson as the Drum Major. A second cast, a few days later, included Jess Walters as Wozzeck, Max Worthley as the Captain, Frank Sale as the Drum Major and Otakar Krauss as the Doctor. The conductor was Erich Kleiber, whose handling of the score was universally praised: 'No score of like modernism has been played to us with such intimacy, such fine gradings and mouldings and such vibrant feeling', wrote the editor of *The Musical Times*;[43] 'Under his guidance the orchestra played Alban Berg's intricate score as though they had been familiar with it for years, caressing the slender wisps and tendrils of melody and preserving that sensuous beauty of sound without which the composer's intention cannot be realised', said Desmond Shawe-Taylor in the *New Statesman*.[44] Caspar Neher's sets were regarded as adequate ('unassertive and individual', said *The Musical Times*; 'striking, if less succesful than one might have hoped', said the *New Statesman*), and the pro-duction by Sumner Austin safe (if 'dull and lacking in tension'). Amongst the cast only Christel Goltz was generally criticized for her too 'tough conception' of Marie:

Christel Goltz, sprawling across the table or lunging menacingly towards the child, turned her into a hard-boiled garrison tart. By an unhappy coinci-dence her Drum Major. . .evinced a comical lack of virility in a part which demands little else, so that the scene of her seduction by him made a topsy turvy effect.[45]

The main concerns of the British critics were not the musical struc-tures of the opera (as had been those of their German colleagues) but the viability of *Sprechgesang* when applied to the English language ('neither song nor talk, it sometimes fails even to achieve its declared purpose of reproducing the accents and contours of ordinary speech', said Ernest Newman, the doyen of English critics of the time;[46] '"Sprechgesang", that unsatisfactory half-way house between speech and song, is a German invention and is apt to sound odder still in any other language' said Shawe-Taylor). Perhaps because of their unfamiliarity with German expressionism, they wondered also whether *Wozzeck* was not too depressing to qualify as great art.

Most critics agreed with William Mann, who observed that 'It is a drama of low life, hallucination and sordidness, yet over the whole work hovers an aura of nobility.'[47] Some critics felt differently: 'It would be futile to deny that dramatically something is wrong', wrote Winton Dean in *Opera*: 'The objection to the chief characters is not that they are squalid or morally repulsive but that they are so unbalanced by insanity as to destroy the dramatic standard by which their behaviour can be measured. [In the 'repulsive' Act II scene 2] the spectacle of two madmen tormenting a third is artistically not horrifying but tedious.'[48] John Amis, writing in *The Musical Times*, found the experience depressing: 'I felt as though I had lost about a quart of blood. *Wozzeck* is immensely lowering to the spirit without having the cleansing quality of catharsis. Should great art be lowering? I say no. . .I don't want to undergo another *Wozzeck* for a decade or two. . .I don't want my emotions dragged through sink and gutter.'[49] Martin Cooper, in *The Spectator*, wrestled with the same problem:

What of the value of the work itself? Nobody can question the composer's musical and dramatic genius; he not only creates the exact musical equivalent for each scene but in details of orchestration and dynamics, in his choice of melodic fragments and his subtle references to popular music he is a consummate artist. Are these gifts wasted on the illustration of a nightmare, on a piece which – as one penetrating critic has suggested – is nearer to Grand Guignol than to tragedy? No lover of opera will object to a very high proportion of bad characters on stage but what are we to make of a piece in which so many are mad, and where the composer himself exerts all his gifts to emphasise the unreal hallucinatory quality of the drama and the characters? If Wozzeck and his tormentors were sane, our emotions would be stirred rather than our nerves lacerated; but if they were sane would Berg have found such apt and potent musical expression for them?

And so we return to how much the subject matter of a work of art affects its value. The champions of 'art for art's sake' will claim that for them only aesthetic distinctions are to be made between, say, *Fidelio* and *Wozzeck* or Baudelaire's *Une Charogne* and St Bernard's Hymn to the Virgin from the

Paradiso – that all that matters is the perfect realisation of the artist's conception, no matter what that conception may be. And in that case *Wozzeck* is certainly superior to *Fidelio*. Only what a narrowing down of art this implies! Convenient and comforting, no doubt, when we have seen art enslaved to moral or political ends, but surely too easy a way out – a divorce from life which is indeed a decadence, a falling-away from the great achievements of the past.[50]

If Cooper was the most eloquent of the critics in giving voice to the worries which lay behind many British notices of *Wozzeck*, by far the most irascible was W. R. Anderson, who reviewed the broadcast of the Covent Garden production for *The Musical Times*. Having dealt (unusually for the British press) with the 'too complex forms' (which, said Anderson, 'can scarcely be distinguished') and the problems of *Sprechgesang* (which he thought a 'worn-out and tiresomely limited' device), Anderson went on to comment:

Berg's music is almost beyond criticism. . .but the work remains for me the second most horrible opera in the world, and by far the cleverer of those two (the other being that revolting humbug *Jenufa*). If opera has ceased to be a pleasant nonsense-tale set to music it ought to get much more criticism and analysis of plot, motive and mentality. . .I'm afraid that there is a tendency to be dazzled by strange and powerful music which few can claim to take in fully. . .It occurs to me that more people might enjoy the work as a ballet; though far be it from me, who care very little for this over-whooped art, to suggest that still more victims should be cast to the lions. . .it might be that powerful miming could convey at least as much meaning as the words do and maybe deepen the significance of this fumbling social document. . .musically it holds nothing to comfort the heart.[51]

If the London premiere of the opera was generally recognized as a triumph and a major event in British musical life in the early 1950s, the first New York production of *Wozzeck* (excepting, that is, the guest performance given by the visiting Philadelphia company in 1931) was, in production terms at least, little short of a disaster. Staged by the New York City Opera Company and conducted by Joseph Rosenstock, the company's new general director, the production opened on 3 April 1952. The title part was sung by Marko Rothmüller, the London Wozzeck who had flown over for the occasion. *Opera* reported that although the New York critics 'were divided as to his [Rothmüller's] vocal merits' they 'were virtually unanimous in condemning the production by Komisarjevsky and the settings of Dobujinsky, both of which gave the piece a feeling of Russian realism instead of German expressionism'.[52] Reviewing the production in *Musical America*, Robert Sabin observed that, although much credit was due to the orchestra and singers for 'a devoted, often eloquent interpretation',

Theodore Komisarjevsky's production and stage direction revealed a miscomprehension of both the content and the style of the opera and Mstislav Dobujinsky's scenery was almost equally inappropriate. The musical excellences of the performance were often obscured by arbitrary, sometimes outrageous, details of staging that distorted the flow of the action and killed the magic of Frederick [*sic*] Büchner's play. . .Mr Komisarjevsky and Mr Dobujinsky have given us a fussy, literalistic, crude production that misses that whole point of the tragedy. The two-level unit stage is crowded with ugly details. . .to get at her window Marie has to rush out a doorway at lower stage left and climb to what looks like a coal opening near the floor of the upper stage. . .the current production is so excellent musically, despite limitations of means, that Mr Rosentock might well abandon the set and perform the opera with curtains, a few painted drops and lights. It would be infinitely more effective done thus than in its present garish and inept staging.[53]

Rosenstock took the critics' advice and the production was withdrawn after a few performances.

By this time European opera companies had recovered from the effects of the war and there were now many productions of *Wozzeck* in preparation. Productions in Milan and Vienna opened later in 1952, in Kiel, Oldenburg, Hamburg and Wiesbaden in 1953, in Heidelberg in 1954 and in Hanover, Kassel and Wuppertal in 1955.

The year 1955 also saw one of the most significant post-war revivals of the opera when on 14 December, thirty years to the day after its premiere, *Wozzeck* returned to the stage of the Berlin Staatsoper. The conductor was the veteran Johannes Schüler, who had conducted the first provincial production of the work in Oldenburg in 1929. Although *Opera* greeted the production by Werner Kelch and the 'excellent sets' by Hainer Hill with enthusiasm (while observing that Kurt Rehm's Wozzeck illustrated 'the crucial point of the Staatsoper situation: its dearth of top-rank voices'[54]), the real significance of the production was political rather than musical. Rebuilt after the war, the Staatsoper on Unter den Linden, the theatre in which Kleiber had conducted the first performance of *Wozzeck* in 1925, was now in the part of the city that was under Russian control. Since performances of *Wozzeck* were banned in the Soviet Union, the authorities in charge of the East Berlin Staatsoper had both to defend their decision to mount the piece and, at the same time, distance themselves from a kind of music that was still regarded with official disproval. With this in mind, the programme booklet for the production is a fascinating political document. In an introductory essay on Büchner and Berg, Professor Hans Meyer emphasizes the value of *Wozzeck* as a document of social criticism and the humanitarian ideals which motivated the composer:

Alban Berg was a deeply humanistic composer. While, as Hanns Eisler has observed, most of the operatic and cantata texts chosen by his teacher Schoenberg demonstrate a poor taste in literature, Berg is not only a refined connoisseur of literature but an artist to whom, when he composes, the humanistic content is of importance. His heart, like that of Büchner, beats for those who suffer or are oppressed: it was thus that he could set to music the inhuman game which drives the poor Wozzeck onwards and it is thus that he later approaches the feminist tragedy of Wedekind's *Lulu*.

In an essay on the music the composer Paul Dessau (one of Brecht's close collaborators) draws on the writings of Stalin and Engels in his attempts to address the questions 'What is atonality? Must it sound "nasty"? And must it be "formalistic"?':

'Our life finds itself in "perpetual motion" and we must therefore study life in its motion' says Stalin (in 'Anarchy or Socialism'). And as a result of such study it must be said that the moments of tension, which I should like to call dissonances, are nothing other than those oppositions without which there is no music, no art and no life itself. 'As soon as there is no opposition there is no life: death enters', says Friedrich Engels.

Having argued the validity of this new musical language, however, Dessau is eager to assure his audience that this language has proved to be an artistic cul-de-sac:

Developments have not stood still since the appearance of *Wozzeck*. Just as this work grew naturally, so did others and so will new ones grow. To us present-day composers, we composers who are seeking new forms and have set new goals, much in Alban Berg's *Wozzeck* seems incapable of being further developed. I believe that the overheated musical language and psychological nature of expressionism have now moved beyond their high-point. Something else has become much more important, namely the inclusion of simple melodies and rhythms that have their origins in the people. The decorative excess of the stylistic tendencies of that period have already made way for a clearer, more direct speech.[55]

Conducted by Karl Böhm, with Hermann Uhde and Eleanor Steber in the main roles, *Wozzeck* finally reached the stage of the Metropolitan Opera on 5 March 1959. All the reviewers were agreed on Böhm's masterly handling of the orchestra (the members of the orchestra were said to have had an unprecedented twenty-four rehearsals and to be able to play the score in their sleep), although

Opera had reservations about the 'overall conception which lacked the plastic sweep and urgency that characterized Erich Kleiber's great Covent Garden performance of 1952'.[56] Most reviewers agreed on the adequacy of Herbert Graf's staging and Caspar Neher's sets (both *Opera* and *Musical America* commented on the extent to which the designs drew on those for the Salzburg and London productions). Ronald Eyre in *Musical America*, however, thought the 'subtle and complex implications' of this 'grim story' too much for 'the tabloid world of opera' and the work too dependent on foreknowledge and preparation on the part of the listener.[57]

A number of reviewers also remarked on the fact that, though an artistic triumph, the production was far from a financial success. Irving Kolodin wrote in *The Saturday Review*:

In putting all its resources at the disposal of Alban Berg's masterpiece Rudolf Bing has discharged a debt, closed a file of unfinished Metropolitan business and, perhaps, opened a vista of operatic things to come. Whether he has, in the process, incurred some debts of a strictly monetary sort will be better known after the scheduled repetitions (the $25 top for the benefit performance left half the orchestra unsold and a hurried call for 'volunteers' to fill the empty seats). But there are times when even a business-minded opera management must be content to take the credit and let the cash go.[58]

Time magazine, in its own inimitable literary style, began its review by declaring that

Manhattan's Victorian red-and-gilt Metropolitan Opera House was transformed one night last week into a nightmarish, shriekingly demented world of sight and sound. The occasion: the Met's long overdue production of *Wozzeck* by the late, famed atonalist Alban Berg. It was one of the great nights in Met history.

Observing that 'the fear that American audiences were not ready for *Wozzeck*'s cerebral, atonal music long discouraged the Met from attempting it', *Time* also noted that *Wozzeck* 'moved Manhattan critics to shouts of praise and touched off the most clamorous standing ovation of the current season. But on opening night (a benefit with a $25 top) nearly 1,000 seats were empty in a heavily papered house and there is virtually no demand for tickets for the remaining performances this season. The Met will not present *Wozzeck* next year. A quarter-century after his death Composer Berg still seems to be a generation ahead of the times.'[59]

Although *Wozzeck* now occupies a permanent place in the repertoire, it remains a difficult opera to mount and an opera that makes unusual demands on the vocal and dramatic abilities of the performers and on the production team as a whole. Perhaps the most difficult, and certainly still the most contentious, musical decision to be taken concerns the performance of the *Sprechstimme*. In the instructions printed at the front of the vocal and orchestral scores of the opera, Berg comments that in this 'rhythmic declamation':

The melodies in the vocal part which are distinguished by special notes are not to be sung. The performer has the task of changing them into a spoken melody while taking into account the pitch of the notes. This is achieved by:
1. adhering very precisely to the rhythm (and note values), allowing no more freedom than in normal singing.
2. being aware of the difference between singing and speaking voices: in singing the performer stays on the note without change: in speaking he strikes the note but leaves it immediately by rising or falling in pitch but always bringing out the relative pitches of the notes.

The performer must take great care not to fall into a singing manner of speaking. This is not what the composer intends: nor does he desire a realistic, natural manner of speaking. On the contrary, the difference between ordinary speech and speech that can be used in music should be clear. On the other hand there should be no suggestion of singing.

Berg amplified these remarks in his 1930 essay 'The preparation and staging of "Wozzeck"':

No singing under any circumstances! Still, the pitches are to be stated and held exactly as indicated by the notes, but held with the tone of the speaking voice. To be sure, such a speaking voice need not be restricted to chest tone throughout. Head tones are also possible, even necessary, since the normal speaking voice is often too low and of too limited a compass. For this reason these spoken pitches are placed where they will cause the singer no more difficulty or harm than the sung tones suitable to the different registers and to various changes in expression.

Only in those cases where, in spite of these directions, an unnatural and mannered timbre (either in the high or low registers) is unavoidable, is it permitted to execute the spoken melody in a narrower compass, within which, however, 'the relationship of the individual pitches to one another must be absolutely maintained.'[60]

Despite these detailed instructions, the precise manner in which Berg intended the *Sprechstimme* to be realized (and, indeed, whether it can be realized at all) remains a matter of contention. Boulez, for one, believes that the *Sprechstimme* remains a 'problem that will never be solved really satisfactorily', since Berg's demands rest on 'a mistaken analysis of the relation between the speaking and the singing voice':

In some performers the tessitura of the singing voice is more extensive and higher in pitch than that of the speaking voice, in which the range is smaller and the pitch lower. On the other hand many singers have a very similar tessitura (after all, voices are trained in order to achieve certain 'norms') but the tessitura of their speaking voice is quite different – and this is particularly true of women, so that passages of *Sprechgesang* can be both too high and too low for them. Finally the speaking voice ceases to sound because its actual emission is short. You might say that the pure speaking voice is a kind of percussion instrument with a very short resonance – hence the impossibility of pure speaking tone of long duration.[61]

It is perhaps worth observing that the experience of recordings and performances of *Wozzeck*, other than those of Boulez's, suggests that the *Sprechstimme* is not as insoluble a problem nor Berg's demands as unrealistic as the above comments suggest.

Berg's opera also makes particular and unusual demands on the production team, for few operas (and perhaps no other opera apart from Berg's own *Lulu*) offer less scope for 'creative' directorial additions. 'The function of a composer is to solve the problems of an ideal stage director', says Berg in 'A word about "Wozzeck"', and in both *Wozzeck* and *Lulu* Berg has mapped the most important stage directions into the score. Indeed the correlation between what happens on stage and what happens in the orchestra is so close and so carefully worked out that any over-ingenious bits of stage business or interpretative ideas that a director introduces are likely only to run counter to Berg's express wishes or to contradict what is going on in the music.

This has, of course, not stopped directors from trying to impose their own idiosyncratic interpretation on the piece. It has recently become fashionable (the trend seems to have been started by Pierre Boulez) to present the opera as a single unbroken act. This practice, presumably initiated because it was thought to enhance the dramatic power of the piece, not only destroys the effect of Berg's $5+5+5$ symmetrical structure but, more importantly, makes pointless the carefully-worked-out links between the end of one act and the beginning of the next – the musical relationship between the alternating chords that close Act I and, in a different guise, open Act II; the dramatic relationship between the curtain which ends Act II and opens Act III. In Britain we have recently had a production of *Wozzeck* by Scottish Opera (1980) which not only ignored Berg's specific directions about the way in which the curtains were to be handled but had sets which made observance impossible, since the falling curtain was replaced by a sheet suspended from wire and run across the stage by a stage hand. We have also had a production from

Welsh Opera (1986) in which the orchestral interludes were reduced to background music accompanying action devised by the producer and in which a newly invented 'coup-de-théâtre' was added after Berg's opera had ended. When such basic elements of the musical and structural design of the opera are ignored, it is, perhaps, hardly surprising that the more subtle correspondences between music and action should count for little in such productions – that, as in the recent Covent Garden revival for example, the tension and irony of the scene with the Doctor, when the two obsessions confront one another, should be dissipated by having the Doctor surrounded by a rowdy group of medical students.

In his essay 'The preparation and staging of "Wozzeck"'[62] Berg observes that there are some scenes in the opera which 'from the point of view of stage directions are more freely composed' and in which 'the fantasy of the producer is given much greater leeway'. His examples make it clear that he regarded the permissible limits of such directorial 'freedom' and 'fantasy' as being severely circumscribed: 'For example, in the scene in the Doctor's study it would not be unsuitable to have the action made more lively by a medical examination, temperature taking etc. in keeping with and parallel to the dialogue. Similar liberties may be taken in the two tavern scenes.'[63] In the new (1987) production at the Vienna Opera, this very scene is 'livened up' not by the Doctor taking Wozzeck's temperature, as Berg modestly suggested, but by the Doctor carrying out a full-scale urinalysis – complete with test tube, alcohol lamp, pipette and well-filled specimen bottle – on-stage.

Wozzeck, like all great operas, can withstand, and remain effective in spite of, such things. The pity is that by imposing their own crude and often vulgar readings on the piece such productions conceal, if not destroy, the subtlety and sophistication of Berg's own musico-dramatic conception.

1 Piano Sonata No. 4 in D minor. One of five piano sonatas which Berg began while studying with Schoenberg. The opening bars of the abandoned fourth sonata became the opening bars of the final orchestral interlude of *Wozzeck*. (Music Department, Austrian National Library, MS F 21/Berg 48)

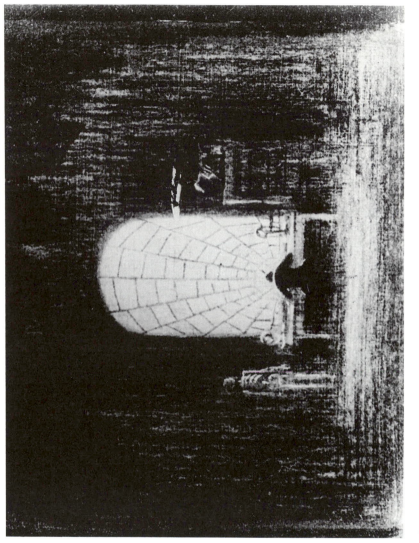

2   Berlin, December 1925. Sketch by Panos Aravantinos for the set of Act I scene 4 (Universal Edition)

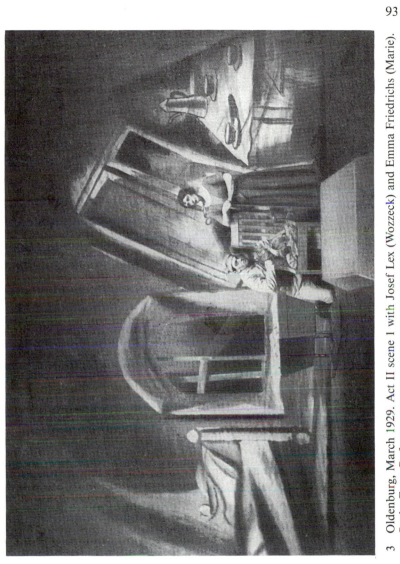

3   Oldenburg, March 1929. Act II scene 1 with Josef Lex (Wozzeck) and Emma Friedrichs (Marie). Set by Ernst Rufer

4   Aachen, February 1930. Berg with members of the cast and the production staff. L. to R.: Heinrich Strohm (director), Helmut Jürgens (designer), Berg, Richard Bitterauf (Wozzeck), Alice Bruhn (Marie), Paul Pella (conductor)

5 Aachen, February 1930. Act II scene 3. Richard Bitterauf (Wozzeck),
Alice Bruhn (Marie)

6   Aachen, February 1930. Act II scene 5. Richard Bitterauf (Wozzeck), Anton Ludwig (Drum Major)

7 Aachen, February 1930. Act III scene 2. Richard Bitterauf (Wozzeck), Alice Bruhn (Marie)

8 Darmstadt, February 1931. Lothar Schenk von Trapp (designer). Act I
scene 2. Albert Lohman (Wozzeck), Johannes Schocke (Andres)

9   Darmstadt, February 1931. Act II scene 1. Anita Mittrovic (Marie)

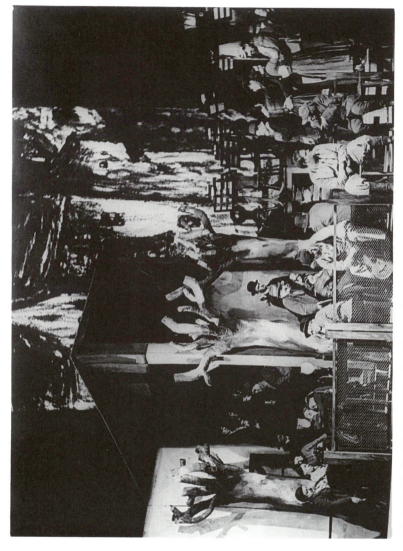

10 Darmstadt, February 1931. Act II scene 4

11 Darmstadt, February 1931. Act II scene 5. Albert Lohman (Wozzeck),
Joachim Sattler (Drum Major)

12 Philadelphia, March 1931. Sketch by Robert Edmund Jones for Act I
scene 4 (Universal Edition)

13   Frankfurt, April 1931. Ludwig Sievert (designer). Act III scene 2. Jan
     Stern (Wozzeck), Erna Recka (Marie) (Universal Edition)

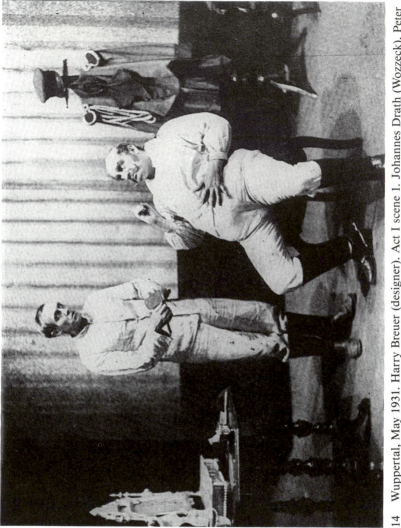

14 Wuppertal, May 1931. Harry Breuer (designer). Act I scene 1. Johannes Drath (Wozzeck), Peter Markwort (Captain)

15 Wuppertal, May 1931. Act II scene 2. Johannes Drath (Wozzeck), Peter Markwort (Captain), Walter Hagner (Doctor)

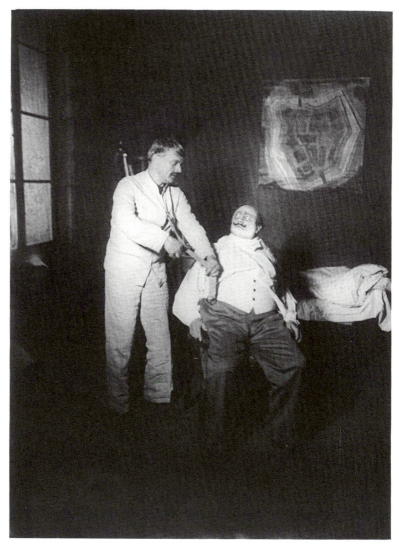

16   Leipzig, October 1931. Walter Brugmann (designer). Act I scene 1. Karl
August Neumann (Wozzeck), Reiner Minten (Captain)

17 Leipzig, October 1931. Act II scene 2. Karl August Neumann (Wozzeck), Reiner Minten (Captain), Ernst Osterkamp (Doctor)

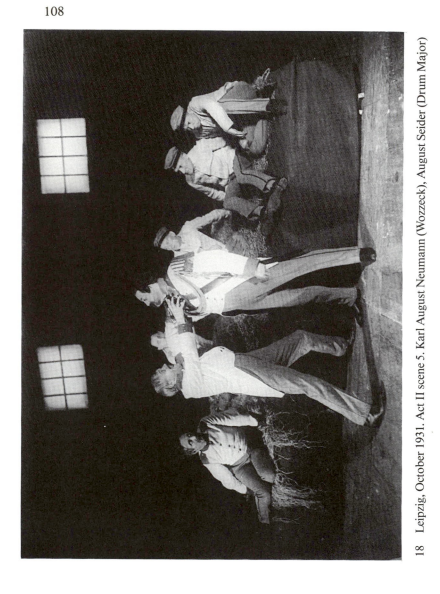

18　Leipzig, October 1931. Act II scene 5. Karl August Neumann (Wozzeck), August Seider (Drum Major)

19   Zurich, October 1931. Sketch by Karl Groening-Altona for the set of Act III scene 2

Documents

Of the nine documents reprinted in the following section two are entirely concerned with the Büchner play.

The first, by Karl Emil Franzos, is a vivid description of the innumerable problems with which he had to cope when preparing the first edition of *Woyzeck* for inclusion in his complete critical edition of Büchner's works (published in 1879). The important and little-known document reproduced here, which quotes extensively from Franzos's introduction to the complete edition, is the second of two articles which appeared under the title 'Über Georg Büchner' in 1901 in vol. 29 (pp. 195ff, 289ff) of *Deutsche Dichtung*. The second of these documents is by Hugo Beiber ('Wozzeck und Woyzeck', *Literarisches Echo*, vol. 16, 1 June 1914, pp. 1188ff) and tells of his discovery of the origins of Büchner's play in the published court and medical reports on the case of the real Johann Christian Woyzeck.

The remaining articles are concerned with the Berg opera. The first two were both written by people closely associated with Berg. Erwin Stein studied with Schoenberg in Vienna from 1906 to 1910 and, like his close friends Berg and Webern, was one of the 'Vortragsmeister' of the Verein für musikalische Privataufführungen. His 'Alban Berg and Anton Webern' (first published, interestingly enough, in English in *The Chesterian*, no. 26, pp. 33–6 in October 1922) appeared only a year after Berg had finished the opera and a few months before the score was printed. The article represents what is probably the first mention of *Wozzeck* in the press and also, as far as I am aware, the first time that the names of Berg and Webern were publicly coupled together.

Fritz Heinrich Klein, a pupil of Schoenberg and Berg, prepared the vocal score of the *Wozzeck* and later the piano score of the Chamber Concerto. Himself a composer, Klein is perhaps best known to admirers of Berg as the inventor of the so-called 'Mother chord' and, in its horizontal manifestation, the note-row which Berg used in the song 'Schliesse mir die Augen Beide' and the first movement of the *Lyric Suite*. Klein's article on *Wozzeck* was published in *Musikblätter des Anbruch*, the house magazine of Universal Edition which had carried Berg's own polemic 'The Musical Impotence of Hanz Pfitzner' in June 1920 and of which he was editor for a short time, in vol. 5, October 1923, pp. 216–19.

Ernst Viebig's 'Alban Bergs "Wozzeck": ein Beitrag zum Opernproblem' appeared in print, in the Berlin periodical *Die Musik*, vol. 15/7, pp. 506ff, in April 1923, before Klein's *Anbruch* article, but is here placed after so that it and the following two articles, by Petschnig and by Berg himself, can be read as a set. Viebig's enthusiastic article, written by someone who, unlike Stein and Klein, was outside Berg's immediate Viennese circle (and who, indeed, did not know the composer personally), gave Berg enormous pleasure. It also provoked the critical article by Emil Petschnig which appeared in the following February edition of the same periodical (*Die Musik*, 16/5, February 1924, pp. 324ff) and which, two months later, drew in turn a response by Berg himself in his 'Die musikalischen Formen in meiner Oper "Wozzeck"' (*Die Musik*, 16/8, May 1924, pp. 587ff).

The two final items are also by Berg himself. The short 'A word about "Wozzeck"' began life as the second section (entitled 'Pro Domo') of the piece 'Das "Opernproblem"' that Berg wrote for the *Neue Musikzeitung* (vol. 9, Stuttgart) in 1928 and appeared in English under the title it has here in vol. 5 of *Modern Music* in November of the same year. The more extended 'A lecture on "Wozzeck"' is Berg's most substantial comment on the opera and was originally written as a lecture to precede the 1929 Oldenburg performance of *Wozzeck*, although Berg also delivered it on many subsequent occasions. The lecture, which is here published in a new translation, first appeared in Hans Redlich's 1958 book on Berg and has long been out of print and unavailable in English.

1. Georg Büchner

by Karl Emil Franzos

In 1867, when I was still a schoolboy, Georg Büchner's *Dantons Tod* happened to fall into my hands. The impression on me was similar to

that which Lenz had made shortly before. I was transported and enraptured. This impression grew and deepened when I re-read both writers during my years at the university. Indeed, an uncritical admiration was replaced by understanding love, which can discern defects but which knows how to interpret correctly. At that time only Goethe and Heine were perhaps dearer to me than Georg Büchner, and equally dear were only a few, all of them realists – namely, the Russians, Gogol, Pavlov, Turgenev. . .the truth is that this sympathy [for Büchner] corresponded to my innermost being, that I myself – I can permit myself to say this since the question of talent is in no way asserted thereby – was a romantic realist. Any reader of these lines who should by chance know my youthful writings (*Jews of Barnow, Moschko of Parma*), and who can therefore compare my early work to the prevailing literature of those days, will understand how strongly drawn I must have felt myself to the romantic realists. . .
I was alone in those days, at first in Graz, and then, from 1873, in Vienna, with my love for Büchner. When I asked a scholar in German literature if he couldn't lend me the *Nachgelassene Schriften*, he replied, 'You must mean Ludwig Büchner, *Kraft und Stoff* [*Force and Matter*]. There isn't any Georg Büchner.' In 1874, long searches in catalogues were required before my book dealer, old Wilhelm Braunmüller at the Wiener Graben, was able to discover and obtain it for me. 'As far as I know', said the old man, smiling, as he handed it to me, 'this must be the most obscure of all German writers. To be sure, in this connection one should never employ a superlative, but I believe he's the one.'
I read everything of Büchner's that was then available, and shortly afterward wrote an essay in which I compared Lenz and Büchner and on the basis of their work – particularly Büchner's splendid novella fragment, *Lenz,* one of the finest things that one writer has ever written about another – tried to show how like-minded Büchner was to his predecessor. I had in the meantime become associated with the *Neue freie Presse*, whose editor-in-chief, Michael Etienne, printed almost everything that I gave him. This essay belongs to the few things that he rejected. He was a man of literary culture and sensitivity, and willing to acknowledge both writers. But a newspaper, in his opinion, ought to deal with only 'two kinds of literature – that which interests people, and that which might interest people'. Büchner and Lenz were as unknown and unread as ever, and the public, which was governed by the prevailing taste, wasn't going to find any pleasure in them, even if they were to read them. The editor-in-chief of the

Vienna *Fremdenblatt*, Herr von Martini, likewise a man of literary culture who was acquainted with both writers, turned the essay down for other reasons. 'These rude fellows', he said to me, 'aren't really writers, since they have no form. We should be glad that we live at a time when, thank God, the artistic form of the drama has finally been established. Why remind us of people who had too little skill and self-discipline to achieve mastery of this form?!' I kept my own thoughts, but the essay remained unpublished.

About a year later a very modest memorial stone for Georg Büchner was to be unveiled at the Zürichberg. The cemetery at Zeltweg, where his bones rested, was to be unlocked. Students of German nationality in the two Zurich colleges had arranged for the writer's remains to be disinterred and newly buried under the 'German Linden' at the Zürichberg. The costs for the memorial stone were provided by the young people, with the assistance of some Zurich professors of German origin. The unveiling was set for 4 July 1875. About fourteen days earlier I chanced upon a notice of this in a Zurich paper. I immediately went to Etienne and asked him to let me write a feuilleton on Büchner for that day. 'Not gladly!' was his reply, 'But since it's so important to you, in God's name – !But wait!' reached for the calendar. 'Right! The fourth of July is a Sunday! Strictly speaking, on a weekday one ought not to dig up an unknown corpse, and on Sunday it certainly wouldn't do!' We agreed that the article would appear on 3 July. I wrote to Ludwig Büchner and asked him for the best sources. He was only able to refer me to the *Nachgelassene Schriften*. I wrote the article and sent it to Etienne. It didn't appear on the third of July. Dismayed, I turned up before Etienne that morning. 'It's coming', the amiable and warm-hearted man called out, in pretended harshness, as soon as I entered. The essay had pleased him, and he therefore wanted to do everything possible, on his part, to bring attention to it. 'It certainly won't do any good!' he continued, in his good-natured, mischievous way. 'You're talking into the wind! At a time when the great ones are Ebers, Wolff, and Lindau, you try to bring Büchner back to life?! Even if you write until you fingers are numb, it won't help!' With this delightful prognostication he sent my article to press for the Sunday edition.

This was the first of the more than forty articles on Georg Büchner that I've published. I could be pleased with the success of the cause that I wished to serve. A number of letters came in to the editor. One of them joked that my special subject now seemed to be crudity –

first crude people, then crude writers. The others, however, wanted to know the price of the book. Old Braunmüller said to me in astonishment, 'Heavens! I've had orders for two copies. The publisher will have a heart attack from surprise and joy!' Though fortunately that didn't happen, his accountant, three years later, told me how astonished they were when forty orders suddenly came in, whereas until then barely two to three copies were sold per year – and almost all of them from Austria. In July 1875, however, I thought it was time to strike while the iron was hot, and I pressed Etienne for such a long time that he accepted a longer article on the unveiling of the tombstone, which Ludwig Büchner had submitted at my suggestion. Etienne did this unwillingly, since he had an aversion to Ludwig Büchner's ways and once described his point of view in a leading article as 'meat-axe philosophy'. This all-too-gross, though not inapt expression, was thereafter much quoted. Etienne took pride in the fact that it originated with him.

Ludwig Büchner wrote me a letter of thanks for my essay from Darmstadt shortly afterwards (10 July 1875), in the warmest phrases imaginable. . .The letter culminated in the request that I occupy myself further with the poet.

In my reply I thanked him for his friendly judgment of my work and assured him that I would confidently dare to intercede further for the poet – it was something close to my heart – so far as any opportunity would present itself. At the same time I inquired about the manuscripts and letters that were mentioned in the Introduction to the *Nachgelassene Schriften*, but that were not included in that edition, and whether or not they were still in possession of the family.

The reply indicated that since 1850, that is, in the preceding twenty-five years, Ludwig Büchner had not occupied himself with the legacy, nor had any other member of the family found time to do so. He therefore couldn't give me any precise information as to what might still be available. However, what was extant in 1850 would presumably still be there and would be made available to me at my request.

Thereupon I requested shipment of the materials.

At the end of 1875 I received a whole heap of packets full of manuscripts. Ludwig Büchner's accompanying letter (Darmstadt, 29 July 1875) explained that this was all of the legacy that was still in his possession. Other things would probably still be in the possession of the author's fiancée, Fräulein Jaegle.

The postage hadn't been prepaid and cost a pretty sum, since in Austria at that time a very considerable surcharge was levied. I have to affirm, however, that I was much less troubled over this unanticipated lightening of my purse, even though I was then a young struggling writer, than I was over the contents of the letter and packets. 'It would really have been in order', I thought, 'if Dr Ludwig Büchner had spent the postal costs of about fifteen marks in sending me his brother's literary remains, with which I'm to occupy myself at his request, so that there's no bias due to family connections; whereas I now have to pay four times as much – but perhaps he forgot about it, although he might easily have thought of it. There is something else, however, to which someone has had to give some serious thought and which he hasn't forgotten, that troubles me much more. That is the conclusion of his letter!' For this conclusion read, word for word, as follows: 'Should you be willing to add some notes concerning the presently surviving Büchner family at the close of your articles, I am prepared to make the necessary material available in due course.'

This made a quite disagreeable impression on me. I was to supply, at the close of every essay on Georg's work and to every notice regarding his literary remains, an advertisement for his three literary siblings, Ludwig, Luise, and Alexander. The 'necessary material' would be made available. If I were to do it people would wonder how I could have such atrociously bad taste as to conclude my essays with such notices, and if I were not to do it the three siblings would certainly not take it favourably. And I would probably need them for the sake of the project, for in editing a literary legacy one is continually dependent on communications with and investigations conducted by the family. What was to be done? When I showed the letter to Etienne, he said, with grim mockery, 'I congratulate you upon your appointment as lecturer on meat-axe philosophy! However, please be so obliging as to present your lectures elsewhere than in my newspaper.'

For the time being this was *cura posterior*. But something else that had to be my immediate concern was the abominable condition of the legacy. It had obviously been put away in an attic, in a poorly protected container, exposed to dust, rain, and mice, and then, just as it was, stuffed into packets – the dust and mouse-droppings had not even been completely removed. Moreover, the contents hadn't been sifted, and so several pounds of old newspapers of the 50s were included. A portion of the manuscripts, namely the school notebooks and several of the philosophical writings, had been gnawed by the mice or were mouldy. Even the manuscripts that were still intact had suffered from dampness and gave off a dreadful odour. In my enthusiasm I had informed the good old woman, a midwife in Mödling near Vienna, from whom I was renting a furnished room at the time, of the treasure I was awaiting. Hardly able to read and write, she nevertheless understood that it concerned the literary remains of a long departed youth who might have achieved, had he lived longer, as much as old Herr von Grillparzer, who lived in the Spiegelgasse in Vienna and whom she still knew by sight and revered. In order to provide a respectable shelter for my treasure she had cleared a small chest and placed it in my room, after carefully scrubbing the drawers and lining them with paper. But now, when the packets arrived and I opened them in her presence, her honest, plump, and wrinkled face got longer and longer, and finally she categorically declared, 'I won't put up with such filth! You'll either throw the things out or – !' I had to plead with her for a long time and to placate her before she finally consented to tolerate me together with the 'filth' in her clean and tidy house, and then she even willingly assisted me in cleaning the papers, but only 'on condition', she remarked. What that 'condition' was she didn't say at first. When we were quite finished, two days later, she brought a little bundle of papers, carefully wrapped in a silk cloth, out of her room. They were the birth, marriage, and death certificates of her family. 'Are there any specks of dust or mouse-droppings?' she asked. 'No, Frau Brunner.' 'And what am I? An educated woman?' I was silent. 'And did my people ever write anything, like Herr von Grillparzer?' This, too, I could confidently deny. 'And what is the gentleman in Darmstadt?' 'A famous author.' 'Then write to him that he ought to be ashamed of himself for the way he has kept his brother's papers, he should be thoroughly ashamed of himself! That is my condition, the – the gentleman must know that I, old Brunner, say this to him!'

I have since been entrusted with the literary estate of several writers. None was in such a condition, none of the donors demanded notices about the 'surviving family', and not a single shipment was – unstamped! This first, sad experience has, fortunately, remained the only one.

Unfortunately, I could not fulfil the condition laid down by honest old Brunner, who worked so lustily and selflessly to clean the manuscripts. . .On the contrary, I gratefully informed Dr Ludwig Büchner of the receipt of the manuscripts and promised to employ them faithfully for the furtherance of Georg Büchner's reputation. I have fully kept that promise.

I set to work eagerly preparing an inventory of the manuscripts and putting them in order. I was troubled that so much was missing, in particular that no letters of any sort at all were included. However, there were some important manuscripts that had never been made use of before, the most significant among them the fragment, *Wozzeck*.

I have already reported in the preceding instalment that this fragment remained unpublished for forty years, even though the author rightfully placed special value on this work, because neither Karl Guzkow, nor Georg Zimmermann, nor, finally, Ludwig Büchner, could, or would, muster the patience, time, and effort required to decipher it. This was the most difficult part of my task and I therefore attacked it first of all. In my edition of Büchner's works (pp. 202ff) I've told how my work on this progressed. I will repeat the most important points:

At first, I didn't have the slightest hope that I would succeed in deciphering it. Before me lay four sheets of dark grey, brittle paper, written on in all directions with long lines of very fine, very pale, yellowish strokes. There was not a single legible syllable. In addition, several small sheets of white paper, covered with similar strokes. Since the marks were larger here and the background lighter, here and there a word could be deciphered, but nowhere as much as a whole sentence. At a loss, I leafed back and forth through the pages. Then, by chance, I came upon the chemical formula employed by the Germanisches Museum in Nuremberg for restoring documents. One first brushes the place in question with distilled water, then with sulphate of ammonia. This expedient proved to be effective and for a short time the faded strokes stood out again, coal-black, even in places where the unaided eye could hardly detect a trace of writing. But then a new difficulty emerged: the characters were microscopically small, often with more than thirty words in an average line. I had to reach for the magnifying glass. But even with the aided eye and with the chemically prepared paper, it was difficult enough. For Georg Büchner, when he wrote quickly, had the most illegible handwriting that one can imagine. In comparison with Büchner's streaks, Alexander von Humboldt's hieroglyphics are a model of calligraphy. On top of that there were idiosyncratic abbreviations, etc. In short, it was an indescribably difficult test of endurance. But whatever I deciphered would steel my courage. And so I copied, line for line, first from the large sheets, then from the small white sheets.

Finally I was finished and could survey the result. What I had deciphered were obviously two markedly different drafts of one and the same work. The grey sheets were the older and larger, the white the later and smaller draft of *Wozzeck*. The first contained about twenty scenes, some only indicated, some scantily sketched in, the smallest number worked out. The ordering was altogether arbitrary. Part of the exposition followed the catastrophe, then part of the closing scene was indicated, then the scene with which the piece was probably supposed to open, and so on. The white pages contained only about ten scenes, likewise without any logical order, some of them realizations of such passages as were only sketched in the grey sheets, some of them new fragments. The scenes of the second draft were collectively related to the catastrophe. In the second draft Büchner had altered the names of the characters, and in some instances their situation as well. . .

The wording of the manuscript before us is now literally presented. If a passage was so illegible that I was not able to determine but could only guess its content, I preferred to omit it, rather than to write it in. . .My only guiding principle was to get at the author's intentions. . .As for the ordering of scenes, this was certainly a difficult task since not a single indication was given. . .Not a single syllable was omitted.

The knowledgeable reader will grant that the task was not an easy one. But no one will guess what I found most difficult about it. The greatest and most annoying difficulty was to see into print, just as he had written it, that which Georg Büchner had written and which I had deciphered after months of fatiguing work. And who placed these difficulties in my way, who, in cold blood, demanded of me the irreverence, the dishonesty, of mutilating the dead author's words? The siblings of Georg Büchner, Ludwig, Luise, and Alexander Büchner! And why? Let that be imparted by Ludwig Büchner's own words, for so improbable is it that it might otherwise not be believed!

As early as 8 August 1875, I was able to inform Dr Ludwig Büchner that I would undoubtedly succeed in the deciphering. On 12 August he replied that my communication had 'extraordinarily pleased' him. As a 'matter of course' he would permit publication, 'in whatever form seems suitable to you'. He would also be agreeable to the publication in full of *Der hessische Landbot*, a revolutionary pamphlet of Büchner's. He lamented that in the interval during which no one had troubled himself about the legacy much of it had obviously perished (I had called attention to lacunae in the material), including, particularly, the letters to the family, and closed 'with best wishes for the success of your painstaking work'. In short, everything was in good order.

But only five days later there followed a second, really more noteworthy letter, the chief passages of which follow:

My family has been troubled during the last few days with the thought that the now deciphered dramatic fragment might contain something that could possibly be more or less detrimental to the memory of the deceased. I therefore request that you reassure me, and therewith my family, through a few lines in respect to this. I would be greatly indebted, should this seem appropriate to you, for permission to make a quick inspection of the manuscript. I'm convinced that you will not take this request amiss, in view of the circumstances. The hostility against our family, particularly however, against me, is so great, embittered, and malicious, that we must observe great precaution with regard to this, in order not to put new weapons into the hands of our fanatical enemies. What a thankless business is the fight for truth and for the enlightenment of mankind!

I was astonished. How could the publication be 'more or less detrimental to the memory of the deceased'? It concerned a work, as Ludwig Büchner well knew, on which Georg had set his greatest hopes. He could not regard it, therefore, as poor and uninteresting, quite apart from the fact that I, whose critical insight he extravagantly praised in every letter at the time, had written him that the fragment was the sketch of a work of genius and contained scenes of great beauty. Only a poor work can be disadvantageous to the memory of a dead poet. Should it contain radical ideas or cynicisms and the like, this couldn't induce a 'more or less' sensible judge to 'more or less' disparage the memory of the dead man. Good heavens! Even after the publication of his *Tagebuch*, Goethe remained, for every reader whose five senses were still sound, the great man, both as human being and as poet, and with Büchner's fragment it wasn't a question of some indelicate frivolity but of a work of overwhelming ethical power! This was all empty talk and the family's fear was for itself. How could a work that Georg Büchner had written in 1836 and that a Viennese writer had now deciphered affect Ludwig, Luise, and Alexander Büchner in 1875? Even the 'fanatical enemies' couldn't possibly be that stupid! And if they were, surely the three 'fighters for truth' couldn't truncate, or even suppress, the work of their brother, dead now for forty years, in the hope of thereby disarming them!

I was apprehensive that things would be demanded of me that would go against my conscience. So that I might be able to converse with him, I found an 'appropriate' way to fulfil Ludwig Büchner's demand, since this is what it was, rather than a reasonable request. Had the legacy not been given to me without any restriction regarding rights of censorship? But on the other hand, my still youthful optimism resisted suspicions of discreditable pressure based on unworthy motives. It was a question of the posthumous fame of the most distinguished member of the family. And so I replied that the copy would follow after the completion of the work, but, though I expressed myself politely, left no doubt as to my views.

Ludwig Büchner's reply (22 August 1875) allowed me to hope that he had understood me correctly. The letter closed as follows:

Now still a word of apology regarding my objection, which may indeed have struck you as strange. I didn't do this of my own volition, but rather because of the objections of my relatives. [There followed details which I can't permit myself to quote.] I myself have had the fullest confidence in you ever since the first work you did on Georg, and in the reverence with which you will treat the memory of the long-departed one.

This sounded very reassuring and in my delight I permitted myself to be pleased that he simultaneously sent me a copy of his sister's newly published *Deutsche Geschichte*, both as a review copy for the *Neue freie Presse* and as 'a modest gift in recognition of your friendly efforts on behalf of my brother'. This double purpose of the one copy didn't really seem like an imposing acknowledgment of my efforts, but all the same, I expressed my appreciation.

After completing my work I sent a copy of *Wozzeck* to Darmstadt. When the manuscript was returned, after a time, I naturally turned at once to Ludwig Büchner's accompanying letter, and breathed a sigh of relief. His judgment of the fragment was very cool; it contained 'much that was trivial[!], quite apart from its cynicisms', but that wasn't essential. It was of more importance for me that a strongly expressed complaint about these cynicisms followed this really interesting admission: 'I recall that it was not only the difficulty of deciphering it, but also its content, so far as I could decipher it, that made me decide, at the time, not to include the fragment in the collection of *Nachgelassene Schriften*.' This, I thought, was a remarkable conception of reverence for a departed brother! On his deathbed (1837) Georg had expressed the fervent wish that his *Wozzeck* might not be lost, and in 1850 Ludwig permits the work to remain unpublished because it contains 'cynicisms'. But all the same, it seemed that he did not wish to be obstructive, since the letter concluded: 'I leave it now entirely to your tactfulness and to your friendly disposition, to bring the fragment before the public in the most fitting way and provided with the required explanatory remarks.' We were thus in agreement!

Now I reached for the copy which he had returned, and was first dumbfounded, and then furious. Wherever possible, the cynicisms were converted, in the most malicious way, into something 'respectable', or simply crossed out, and other quite harmless passages were altered without any evident reason. Indignant, I reached for the letter. There stood the one little sentence that I had innocently overlooked: 'I have permitted myself to correct a few spelling mistakes and faulty expressions.' 'Faulty expressions'! These precious words should find their place in the censor's vocabulary, whoever exercises this wretched calling. Georg Büchner writes cynicisms in *Wozzeck* and Ludwig Büchner corrects these cynicisms as 'faulty expressions'!

What was to be done? Etienne, who had read the fragment and at once declared himself ready to publish excerpts of it in the *Neue freie Presse*, advised me, 'Print what Georg has written and write Ludwig a good, plain letter; then you will be protected from similar jokes in going on with your work.' I got different advice from a man living in Darmstadt, whose respect I had earned through my first article on Büchner and to whom I reported all my experiences, with a plea for his opinion on the matter. He was not surprised, he said, for Dr Ludwig Büchner was the doctor of some well-established families, Luise Büchner had connections with the Grand Duchess Alice, and Alexander Büchner, a mere 'honorary professor' at Caen, had not as yet been definitively rejected for a well-endowed teaching position in Darmstadt. Nonetheless, he opined, Georg Büchner's *Wozzeck* must be printed as he wrote it, but he suggested that since 'vital interests' of the three siblings were involved, they might be appeased through consideration of interests that would seem even more 'vital' to them: I might, for heaven's sake, send for the offered 'material' on 'the surviving family'. Should the surviving family catch sight of the unmutilated *Wozzeck*, they wouldn't blame a man from whom they anticipated publication of this material.

This advice seemed good to me and I followed it. It was, in this case, splendidly ratified. The 'material' arrived (of what it consisted, more later), and when the uncensored *Wozzeck* appeared (in three instalments in the *Neue Freie Presse* in September and October 1875) and was sent to Darmstadt without a covering letter, all that came in return was a polite word of thanks for the information. Only with the publication of *Wozzeck* in my collected edition did the fight begin.

. . .I will point out that Ludwig Büchner himself informed me, in a letter dated 3 October 1875, that at the very beginning of our connection, before I had spoken of a critical collected edition, he had set his eye on arranging this through me and had written to Sauerlaender in Frankfurt am Main. 'I thought at the time', he continued, and I quote this passage literally because it is important for other reasons, 'that I would have to deal with Sauerlaender under any circumstances, though I've since learned that according to German law copyright expires thirty years after an author's death, and his writings then become the property of the state.' The same letter contains the following sentence: 'As far as the second edition of Georg's writ-

ings is concerned, we are half-way in agreement.' Büchner's point of
view on the matter, as repeatedly unfolded in his letters, was as follows: he well knew how inadequate his editing of the *Nachgelassene
Schriften* had been, and he was not unaware that Georg Büchner,
like every true poet, was entitled to the monument of a critical, and
as far as possible, complete edition, though he certainly thought
quite differently than I did about the right of an editor to undertake
alterations. Neither he nor any other member of the family wished to
assume the difficult task. If an outsider was prepared to do this, he
had their blessing, but it ought not to cost them any time or money.
So much to begin with. With reference to the last point, our views
diverged. My position on the matter was that one should not shrink
from any sacrifice of time and effort in order to erect this monument
to Georg Büchner. How much time and effort were necessary I only
saw now, when I could compare the *Nachgelassene Schriften* with
the original manuscripts. And so we really were 'half-way in agreement', and there still remained, at the time, only a single, temporary,
difference. As a title Ludwig Büchner suggested

Georg Büchner's
Nachgelassene Schriften
Expanded and newly edited by K. E. F.
with the kind collaboration and consent of the Büchner family.

I immediately explained, politely but firmly, that I could not go
along with this. One could not say that Georg Büchner's writings
could be 'expanded' by another person; one could not speak of the
'kind collaboration' of the Büchner family, because, in fact, they
were not collaborators. The consent of the family and their willingness to turn the manuscripts over to me I would mention with thanks
in the preface. As title I suggested '*Georg Büchners sämtliche Werke
und handschriftlicher Nachlass*. First critical complete edition. With
an Introduction and edited by K. E. F.' Ludwig Büchner was wise
enough to go along with this at once. He suggested that an honorarium of 600 marks be requested of the publisher.

I approached the laborious task with joy and eagerness. I could
not give all my time and energy to it, but once I had earned the little
that I needed for my living expenses in those days I gave up all the
rest of my time to this work. It soon became clear to me that I would
also have to spend money on it. Of the publishers to whom I turned,
few wanted to know anything about it. Only one made an offer, of
500 marks at first, and finally, 600 marks. Sauerlaender had also

made the same offer through Ludwig Büchner, and since the latter recommended him I agreed that he should arrange the particulars with him. So, it was 600 marks – and the books and material that I had to purchase, and the copies that I had to pay for, cost at least that much. There was no compensation whatever for the work on the edition itself and the writing of the biography. I was satisfied and so informed Dr Ludwig Büchner. My circumstances were known to him.

There then occurred an incident that no one would believe, were I not able, through letters and written agreements, to verify it. When my work on the edition was already far advanced, Dr Ludwig Büchner suddenly wrote to me, 'Of the publisher's fee [the 600 marks from Sauerlaender] I will only claim the approximately 315 francs that the costs of the Zurich memorial came to. The remainder will be compensation for your work.'

I couldn't believe my eyes. Of the 600 marks, which didn't even entirely cover my expenses, I was to give almost half to the famous writer who, through his inheritance, his marriage, and his earnings, had become well-to-do. And yet Dr Ludwig Büchner, as I said, not only knew my circumstances, but also how high my outlay was for purchases and for the expense of copying source materials of the political history of Hesse at the time when Georg Büchner was a member of the conspiracy!

My first reaction was 'No! This is something I won't put up with!' To top it all, I learned at almost the same time, from a report on the erection of the memorial stone in a newspaper which I had ordered from Zurich, that the costs of this had been defrayed by voluntary contributions. His version, therefore, wasn't even authentic. When I became personally acquainted with Ludwig Büchner three years later, I couldn't refrain from asking him just how he had arrived at the figure of 315 francs and what kind of expenses they might have represented. He replied that his and Luise's travelling expenses were high because, once they were in Switzerland, they naturally stayed on for a few days. I was supposed to carry these expenses for a pleasure trip!

. . .I had undertaken this work with such pure and ardent enthusiasm that this episode actually nauseated me. I wanted to be finished with it, not to be haggling about money. So I wrote to Dr Ludwig Büchner that if this seemed right to him I didn't want to argue about it. But I wanted to have peace now, and the satisfaction of being able to see the work through in the way that seemed right to me. And I therefore made it clear to the family that I needed time, that I should not be hurried. This particularly applied to the writing of the biography. This could not be finished quickly, and I also had to reserve the right to publish instalments in advance in newspapers and magazines, which would also bring attention to Büchner. Ludwig Büchner wrote in reply, 'I'm in agreement with everything.'

I continued with my work. Although between July 1875 and October 1876 I devoted an average of at least four hours daily to this, by the late autumn of 1876 I had completed only about twenty proof-sheets of the text and had collected the material for the biography. Anyone who considers the mountain of yellowed, mouldy manuscripts covered with tiny characters that I had to plough through, mainly with the help of the magnifying glass, and what heaps of obscure material (legal documents, political circulars, newspapers, etc.) I had to assemble and to excerpt, will not criticize me for being a slow worker. If I made this impression on Dr Ludwig Büchner, to judge from polite and gentle hints in his letters, this is to be explained, as the correspondence shows, by the fact that he was totally uninformed about the nature of a critical edition. He didn't know, for example, what is understood by a critical commentary, and when he heard of it from me he could not understand what purpose it served and why, for example, where a work was laid out in different manuscripts and editions, these had to be compared line-for-line and an index of textual variants prepared. 'That must be very tiresome', he opined sympathetically, but how much time it required he could not judge. All the same, by November I could give in to the urging of Dr Ludwig Büchner and come to an understanding through him about the details of the contract with Sauerlaender, with whom I had in the meantime personally corresponded as well, since by then the text and supplementary material on Georg Büchner's life lacked only about ten proof-sheets. The contract stipulated that of the honorarium of 600 marks, 400 would fall to me as editor and as author of the biography, and 200 marks to Dr Ludwig Büchner 'as assignee of the editor'. (Publication contract dated 20 December 1876, signed by Dr Ludwig Büchner on 21 December and by me on 23 December.)

. . .The printing was to begin on 2 January 1879. The publisher had arranged this with a printer in Darmstadt. I sent the manuscripts, as usual, to the publisher and was supposed to read the proofs myself. I had, naturally, no objection to Dr Ludwig Büchner seeing the manuscripts in advance: the thought that the fighter for the truth could ever hinder me in my exhausting but successful task of restoring the unmutilated text didn't occur to me in spite of my experience with *Wozzeck*. He had seen that I didn't understand any jokes about such matters. All his efforts to make everything tame and respectable had been in vain. He had finally quietly given in. It was not to be supposed that he would try anything like this again. Everything has its limits! It was the fault of the family that a respectable edition had not been achieved through Gutzkow as early as 1838; it was the fault of the family, or of Ludwig Büchner, that the *Nachgelassene Schriften* was such a bungled piece of work; it was the fault of the family that the literary estate was exposed to mice and mould for twenty-five years; the fault of the family, of their squabble with Minna Jaegle and of the fact that they earned 200 marks from my edition, that this edition did not also include *Pietro Aretino* and the letters – and now would they also try to interfere with a worthy, conscientious edition? It seemed impossible!

But I nevertheless had to experience this impossibility! Shortly after I had sent the first manuscript, that of *Dantons Tod*, to Frankfurt am Main, it was returned to me from Darmstadt. Ludwig Büchner wrote me that Sauerlaender had sent it to him and had complained about the many offensive passages. The most important sentences of Ludwig Büchner's letter are given here in full:

A perusal of the manuscript has persuaded me that you have restored a number of passages that absolutely can't be printed without exposing you, the firm, and us to the most severe reproaches. Besides, these are entirely superfluous for the coherence of the whole and more suited to interfere with the effect of the work of art as such than to enhance it. I have therefore permitted myself, certain of your concurrence in advance, to strike these out again and to change certain all too cynical or vulgar expressions into others that are more suitable or less offensive. I am certain that in doing this I have improved, rather than harmed, the whole.

This went beyond the limits of my patience and I expressed my 'veto' in terms that were admittedly very strong but which I still don't regret having used. I curtly declared that this was not a matter of money but of conscience, and that in this instance I would not yield a jot. There could be no talk of any right of the family to elicit falsifications from me, that in taking on this work I had no purpose other than to correct the offences of the censor in 1835 and of the *Nachgelassene Schriften* in 1850, no purpose other than to procure for the poet, at last, the rights that were his. Why had I been sent the original manuscript if not to publish it? From the beginning of my work the family understood the principles which I had now fulfilled. What right had they now to interfere? This right I would grant to them only if I were to do what Dr Ludwig Büchner had done, if I were arbitrarily to alter the text. What Dr Büchner was now saying, in order to justify his interference, were only the stale phrases of the censor from time immemorial, which were, indeed, always being raked up again. It is up to no one but the poet himself to decide whether or not something interferes with the effect of a work of art. It is of no importance whether these passages do or do not seem superfluous to Dr Büchner. What is important is that Georg Büchner wrote them, and that when they also seemed superfluous to the censor in 1835, he bitterly complained: 'On almost every page something deleted, something added, and almost always in the way that is overall most damaging. The sense is often totally distorted, or quite completely lost and displaced by some insipid nonsense', and so on. In my view it not only takes deplorable boldness to do the same now, in 1877, that the censor did in 1835, but it is also useless trouble. I have no patience for this kind of thing, don't do it myself, and don't tolerate anyone else doing it under my colours. I further emphasized that similar passages were to be found in Shakespeare, Goethe, even in Schiller's *Die Räuber*. All of Grabbe swarms with them. As for the 'severe reproaches' that prigs, prudes, reactionaries, and sanctimonious viragos might raise (the author of *Kraft und Stoff* had also struck out, or replaced by 'more suitable expressions', passages of an atheistic or excessively radical political character), they wouldn't affect me, who would alone carry the responsibility, in the least. No reasonable person would blame the publisher or the family. But granted that the above-mentioned crew should do so, the firm and the family would just have to put up with it. The publisher should have known that Büchner was not a writer for boarding-school girls, and the family was acquainted with the content of the original manuscripts. So, no! no! and again, no!

Ludwig Büchner's reply of 16 January 1877 is very long. I can only give the principal passages here. 'Your very angry letter shows that you are making an error of which I must, above all, disabuse you, if an understanding is to be reached. I didn't know that the original manuscript of *Danton* contained such vulgar and improper obscenities. Perhaps I knew it twenty-eight years ago, when I looked after the publication of the *Nachgelassene Schriften*, but the circumstance has since slipped from my memory. But if I had known it, I should never have guessed or suspected that you would look for the essence of our poet in such things and that you would think of restoring them.' There followed a long explanation that it was only the study of medicine that had led Georg into such 'wayward paths'. 'He would undoubtedly have recognized them later and would have regretted them.' Then an explanation of what a 'work of art' should be – such passages did not belong therein. 'I am almost certain that if they are printed they will bring down a general anathema on our heads, *especially on mine*.' What I had said about other writers wasn't decisive in this case, because 'in this case there *must* be, *without doubt*, respect paid to Georg's *surviving family*.' Moreover, the quarrel between him and me was impractical, 'since if you hold to your point of view an edition on your part is certainly unthinkable, for in all of Germany you won't find a single respectable publisher who will permit his firm to print such things'. This was the first stroke, and the second followed immediately. 'You will certainly not deny that the family, and especially I as its representative, can claim at least the same rights in the edition as you have. It was, after all, I who, with unlimited confidence, supplied you with all the material.' If I would not now permit the family to collaborate in decisions it was self-evident that my position as editor would be terminated.

It is clear how things would have turned out if Ludwig Büchner had continued to be involved: it would have come to a legal action between me and the family, since I would not have been deflected from my right to print the works in the sense of the original agreement, that is to say, in an authentic version. At this point, however, Herr Remy Sauerlaender intervened. He himself informed me of it, and Ludwig Büchner confirmed it. Herr Sauerlaender also found some of these passages disagreeable, but his literary conscience, too, resisted such a gross mutilation as Ludwig Büchner wanted out of concern for the 'general anathema' that the publication would bring down, 'especially on [his] head.' Otherwise very conciliatory to Ludwig Büchner, he nevertheless emphatically made it clear to him that 'respect for the surviving family' could not possibly lead to disrespect for the deceased. In addition Herr Sauerlaender gathered the quite correct impression, from a letter that I simultaneously sent to him, that I would under no circumstances give in, and a lawsuit seemed disagreeable to him. Ludwig Büchner was very, very angry, but it was in vain that he brought to bear the fact of his medical practice in very moral families and of Luise Büchner's connections with the Grand Duchess. Sauerlaender stood fast and they had to give in. And so, immediately after his declaration of war, Ludwig Büchner sent me another communication which ended in a quite different way. He would be satisfied with the elimination of the worst passages and would indicate these provisionally. 'There can be no talk, therefore, of any injury to the poet, and with some good will on your part an understanding can easily be reached.' Would I send him the manuscript again, so that he could show exactly what he would still like to suggest? 'Should my remarks not please you, you're free to take the manuscript back.'

I sent the manuscript, so that I might not seem impolite, but emphasized that I could not deviate from my position.

. . .In the manuscript that now came back to me there were still a dozen alterations. I didn't assent to them, but in order to bring the controversy to an end declared myself ready, of my own accord, not only to assume, in the preface to the edition, sole responsibility for the wording of the text, but also to testify expressly that the family and the publisher had desired modifications.

. . .Since the family now knew that I would yield only on questions of money and that I could not be brought around where it was a question of conscience, one might assume that they would henceforth, at least, have spared themselves and me from similar battles. But not so. The printing of *Leonce und Lena*, where such passages are not found, went smoothly, but with *Wozzeck* the harassment started all over again. . .But what questions these editorial battles concerned! What things we haggled over! The poet permits the swaggering Drum Major to say, 'I'll pound his nose into his a—hole.' That's the way the *Neue freie Presse* and *Mehr Licht* had printed it. But in the book it should say 'into his A—'. I objected that no one would understand this, to which Ludwig Büchner replied that that wouldn't matter in the least! The following correction, on which Ludwig Büchner insisted for the longest time, was even more comical. Wozzeck sees his unfaithful Marie dancing with the Drum Major in the tavern and the poet has him groan: 'Woman! Woman! Go ahead! (Starts up.) How he grabs her! Her body! And she laughs! Damn!' According to Büchner's suggestion the passage should have read: 'How he grabs! And she laughs! Damn!' I replied that in my opinion this made it worse in every way, especially from a 'moral' point of view. . .In his next letter (1 May 1877) he said that he couldn't give in on this point:

To speak frankly, I simply don't understand your point of view about these things. In retaining these vulgarities you don't serve the cause at all, and you hurt yourself and the memory of the poet, who without doubt would have struck these things out had he seen them in the course of correcting the proofs. I hope you won't close your mind to this view. Otherwise, as I've already explained to Sauerlaender, you must expect that I will make a public statement which justifies my and the family's position in this matter and puts the full responsibility on you for these crucial deficiencies.

I replied that he might do whatever seemed right to him; I would fulfil my reverential duty to the dead poet. Which of the two points of view Georg Büchner would have sanctioned may be judged by his aesthetic principles, as well as his letters, which, amongst other things, are filled with blazing wrath against every sort of censorship. . .

'Über Georg Büchner', *Deutsche Dichtung*, 29 (1901), pp. 195ff, 289ff

2. Wozzeck and Woyzeck

by Hugo Beiber

The interesting fragment of a tragedy by Georg Büchner which K. E. Franzos brought to light four decades after the author's death, and which, because of an easily explained misreading, he published under the title *Wozzeck*, has only recently come to be generally appreciated. It has, however, already exercised an important influence on the drama of our day. As to conception, design, and the representation of human character in its mental and spiritual aspect as well as in its conduct, this masterly sketch is an immediate precursor of the strongest and purest works of Gerhart Hauptmann, and its unmistakable influence on Frank Wedekind and Herbert Eulenberg has also been stressed by a number of critics.

There have been repeated attempts to discover the source of this work, which can undoubtedly be traced back to fresh impressions and direct observation of a human being, and attention has been directed to well-known Hessian native types who can still be recalled and who are retrospectively portrayed by Büchner's compatriot, Karl Vogt. As far as I can see, however, it has not heretofore been known that the drama is based on an actual event, which took place during Büchner's childhood and which for some time was of considerable topical interest throughout Germany.

In Leipzig on the twenty-first of June in the year 1821, at 9.30 p.m., the barber Johann Christian Woyzeck, forty-one years old, stabbed his mistress seven times with a broken sword-blade at the entrance to her home. The forty-six-year-old widow of the late surgeon Woost died of the wounds after a few minutes. Immediately after committing the crime the murderer was seized and frankly admitted his guilt. In the course of the inquiry the defence proposed that Woyzeck's mental competence be diagnosed by a forensic physician. This led to two judgments by the Saxon privy councillor at Leipzig, J. C. A. Clarus, a leading authority in the field of psychiatry. Clarus affirmed soundness of mind and supported his opinion with the testimony of witnesses as well as statements by the defendant himself. In addition to the facts already presented, the report included various details that Büchner must have utilized for his Wozzeck (whom we will henceforth call 'Woyzeck') – above all, the fantasy of the Freemasons and the heavenly fire in the second scene.* As to this, Clarus reported the following of Woyzeck: 'While still a journeyman he had heard all sorts of bad rumours about the Freemasons – among other things, that through secret means, for which they only needed a pin, they could kill a man. At the time he didn't believe this, and now he no longer believes it, but he nevertheless always thought about it and tried to imagine the different ways by which the Freemasons might be able to recognize one another. Then he once had a dream: he saw three fiery faces in the sky, of which the middle one was the largest. He connected these three faces with the trinity, and the middle one with Christ because the latter is the greatest person in the Godhead. At the same time he thought that the secret of the Freemasons might also be contained in this number, which was to be revealed to him by this means, and he imagined that the sign of the Freemasons might be the holding up of three fingers.' Thereafter he feared the Freemasons' revenge.

The real Woyzeck also encounters his sweetheart on the dance floor as she dances with a rival. It itself, there would be nothing extraordinary about this and no reason to give it any weight, were it not that in the report Woyzeck related that 'when he was in bed he was full of jealousy, thinking about the church festival and of his mistress there, and he thought he could hear the violins and basses all mixed together, and imputed the words, "On we go! On we go!" to them.' Büchner's Woyzeck likewise repeats the words that Marie

---

* My citation follows the generally available edition of the *Inselbücherei* [the Landau edition] without altogether sanctioning its ordering of the scenes. In particular, I consider it unwarranted to strike out the inn scene with the struggle between Woyzeck and the Drum Major. [Landau took this to be a variant of the barracks scene and printed it as a footnote. Berg combines the two scenes in the barracks scene (Act II scene 5) of the opera.]

had whispered when she danced by with the Drum Major: 'On we go! On we go!' (pp. 26, 29). Finally, to close the chain, Woyzeck, in the report as in the drama, believes that he hears an invisible voice admonishing him, 'Stab the Woost-woman (the she-wolf) to death!' The parallels between these details speak even more strongly than the general correspondence of the overall conception and of the names, which can't be coincidental.

The respects in which Büchner departs from his model are not such as might raise any doubt about the connection, but since they are of some importance for our understanding of the poetic process involved in reshaping the material, we will mention them here. The 'historical' Woyzeck is only occasionally averse to pleasure, amusement, dance, and drink. He has periods of drunkenness, during which he acts crudely and violently. Sometimes he even resigned himself with equanimity to the infidelity of his mistress. He had been in the military service of the Dutch, Swedes, and Mecklenburgers, but at the time of the murder he is no longer a soldier. Above all, Büchner eliminated a critical part of Woyzeck's early history – his abandonment, ten years earlier, of a woman with whom he had had a child. A more detailed discussion as to why a poet concerned with the deepening of character and the concentration of events should have reshaped the story isn't necessary. The conclusion one reaches after repeatedly examining the sources is that what he omitted is certainly more instructive than what he used, but what he retained is not without significance for our understanding.

The decision as to Woyzeck's fate led to a long scientific debate, in the course of which the psychologist Heinroth (the same one whom Goethe thanked for 'bedeutende Fördernis durch ein einziges geistreiches Wort'), amongst others, sided with the Court Physician, while the District Court Physician Marc (from Bamberg) violently polemicized against both.

It is very likely that Büchner would already have heard of Woyzeck's crime when he was still a boy in his father's home, and one can imagine that the sensation caused by this affair in Germany might have made a deep, long-lasting impression. It is also possible that Büchner first came upon it in later years. There can be no doubt that he read the above-mentioned reports, since the 'State Journal for Medicine', edited by Adolf Henke, the 4th and 5th supplementary issues (1825 and 1826) of which carried the report concerning 'the mental competence of the murderer Woyzeck' that is discussed above, counted Georg Büchner's father among its contributors.

In that same journal the latter even discussed at length a case of questionable mental competence involving a soldier who violently attacked a superior.
'Wozzeck und Woyzeck', *Literarisches Echo*, 16 (1 June 1914), pp. 1188ff

3. Alban Berg and Anton von Webern

by Erwin Stein

Alban Berg and Anton von Webern are pupils of Schoenberg. They were, so to speak, present when the Chamber Symphony, the Quartet in F♯ minor and the songs from the 'Buch der hängenden Gärten' were composed; they actually experienced the absolute necessity that gave birth to a new music, and could therefore not help making Schoenberg's style their own. Style, however, is but the *manner* used by the composer to express his *matter*. He may have his manner in common with another artist, but his matter is entirely his own.

The problems of form raised by modern music will be more satisfactorily appreciated in the future. It is enough to point out here that the disuse of the old tonalities and their harmony has inevitably swept away some of the current means whereby symmetry and closeness of form used to be imparted to a piece of music, two factors which the hearer is accustomed to consider as indipensable formal conditions to the perception of a work of art. The dissonant harmony of to-day aggravates the difficulty of recognising musical continuity, and it is therefore easy to understand why so many composers who adopted a new style began by writing pieces approaching dance forms, where symmetry and closeness of form were suggested mainly by repetition and juxtaposition of simple rhythmic motives.

The works of Alban Berg* are symphonic in character. They consist generally of extended movements, where the thematic material is developed polyphonically and in very free variation. This explains, at the same time, their form, which is created by uniformity of the themes and clarity of cohesion. Thus, in his Orchestral Prelude, Op. 6, nearly all the manifold musical occurrences are evolved from a motive of three notes. In other cases, a number of themes are

* Op. 1, Sonata for Piano, Op. 2, 4 Songs, Op. 3, String Quartet, and Op. 5, 4 Pieces for Clarinet and Piano, are published by Haslinger in Vienna and Schlesinger in Berlin. Special attention is drawn to the unpublished orchestral pieces, Op. 6.

placed next to or over each other from the very beginning. Contrasts, which in older music create a sense of symmetry of expression and form in large spaces, are here given a new function: the fact that they appear simultaneously, – that is to say polyphonically – or nearly so, imparts a variety and an extent to the expression within which, as in the human soul, there is room for contradictory notions. The relation between the themes is, at the same time, of so intimate a nature, and they are so compellingly summarized in the working-out, that the whole, although rich in contrasting colours, makes an impression of the greatest unity. In Berg's String Quartet, Op. 3, for instance, three motives of entirely different character are opposed to each other in the first three bars; yet they are related to each other through some formal device or another, such as inversion, augmentation or rhythmic completion, and the development unfolds their affinity: the common experiences of dissimilar relatives. 'Music describes the adventures of themes', as Schoenberg says.

In his most recent work, 'Wozzeck' (after a drama by Büchner), Berg has reinstated a concentrated form of dramatic music. The opera consists of fifteen scenes, each of which is a rounded piece of music. Next to older forms there are numerous formal ideas that have grown out of the new medium. The first act contains five characteristic pieces describing the five principal characters in the drama. The first scene is a Suite (Sarabande, Gigue, Gavotte and Double) in modern style; the second a fantasy on the sequence of three chords; the fourth a theme with twenty-one variations (the Doctor, who in each variation always reverts to the discussion of his science). The five scenes of the second act form a symphony in five movements: a Sonata movement, a Prelude and Fugue on three themes, a *Largo* for chamber orchestra (with the same orchestration as that of Schoenberg's Chamber Symphony), a Scherzo, and a Rondo. The third act contains the following six Inventions: the first on a theme (seven Variations and Fugue); the second on one note (pedal-point); the third on a rhythm (quick Polka for piano); the fourth on six notes (both as chords and resolved into melodic succession); the fifth on a single key (orchestral Interlude in D minor); and the last on a *moto perpetuo* (*quasi Toccata*).

The severe, tense forms of Berg's opera, by reason of the fact that they contain something organically necessary and are thus drama in themselves, create a sense of outward concentration of the dramatic moments. The species and the character of the pieces correspond, needless to say, with the action of each scene, but the wealth of form is equalled by the richness of sound, texture and expression of Berg's melodies. We have before us a master who is leading dramatic music into new paths.

The works of Anton von Webern† are suffused with an extraordinarily tender and intimate feeling. He is the composer of the *pianissimo espressivo*. Most of his pieces are short and extremely transparent in sound, and his melodies are highly, sometimes ecstatically, expressive. In his later orchestral works, strings and wind are used throughout as solo instruments, and the brass is always muted. In the 'Six Movements for String Quartet', Op. 9, almost every note of a melody is given to a different instrument, and each one in a different tone-colour (harmonic, *pizzicato*, *col legno*, etc.). This, together with a rhythm that often lays stress on the weak beat of a bar, imparts to these pieces something unusually glittering and fluid. Schoenberg's idea of a 'melody of tone colour' may have influenced these features. It was a natural consequence of the composer's renunciation of the conventional formal means that these movements could not be allowed to assume large dimensions. They are melodies in one breath. Thematic development, climax and contrast do their share from the very beginning, as it were before the melody has lost its initial warmth. Thus are formed shapes of frequently less than ten bars, but of very concentrated expression. The composer only says the barest essentials, and his expression determines the form of the pieces. There is a Funeral March in the orchestral pieces, Op. 6: bass drum, a peal of bells, kettle drums, a sobbing clarinet melody, bells again, melodic fragments here and there over a march in the trombones, renewed peal of bells, a shrieking outburst of the whole orchestra, a huge *crescendo* for percussion, and the piece breaks off. None of the traditional formal patterns will fit this work, and yet it is a most affecting and closely-knit movement.

Anton von Webern's lastest [*sic*] songs (accompanied by a few solo instruments) are very simple in form. They too show the greatest freedom of melody, harmony and rhythm, but, according to the metre, they are built up more symmetrically, and their expression is often frankly popular in feeling, as for instance in the 'Geistliche Lieder'. In these most mature works of Webern a variety of sound is gained by means of the few instruments, comparable only to Schoenberg.

† Op. 1, Passacaglia for Orchestra, Op. 2, "Entflieht auf leichten Kähnen," for mixed chorus unaccompanied, Op. 3, 5 Songs, Op. 6, Orchestral Pieces, Op. 7, 4 Pieces for Violin and Piano, all published by the Universal Edition in Vienna.

As a consequence of greater wealth of artistic means, the technique of an art is apt to be narrowed down and impoverished in other respects. This is not unnatural, for it is difficult for the ear, while occupied in becoming accustomed to new sounds, to grasp at the same time such things as complex forms. The harmonic richness of to-day is therefore frequently accompanied by simplified melodic and formal conceptions. Schoenberg and his pupils, however, have not only revived the polyphonic principles of the old masters; they have adapted the modifications of motives and development of themes, the thematic and rhythmic variety evolved by the classics, to their new artistic media. This is undoubtedly a great enrichment of musical expressiveness; and if the hearer be unable to follow immediately, he should have patience and accustom himself to this music by hearing it frequently. It will not fail to reveal its musical wealth to him in time.　　　　*The Chesterian*, 26 October 1922, pp. 33–6

4. Alban Berg's 'Wozzeck'

by Fritz Heinrich Klein, Vienna

Seldom have the words 'for the first time' been used with such deep significance on the play-bill of a premiere as in the case of the opera 'Wozzeck', which in its form and its musical spirit has truly created something 'for the first time'. For Berg has written not an internationally conventional 'music drama' but an opera with a completely new kind of structure in which the themes, springing from the dramatic situation, undergo a formal musical development and in which the opera itself is divided into sections which include almost all the forms of absolute music. In order to make the fusion of dramatic and absolute music thus achieved more understandable I would like to describe briefly the formal structure of the opera and the way it develops out of the plot.

The opera consists of three acts each of which contains five scenes. In the first act, the central figures are presented through character studies. First of all the Captain, whose conversation with Wozzeck (who is shaving him) fluctuates between assumed benevolence and arrogant superiority, is represented in a Suite consisting of a Prelude, Sarabande, Cadenza for viola, Gigue, cadenza for double bassoon, Gavotte with two Doubles, Air and a retrograded reprise of the Prelude. A finale section, which acts as the development of the Suite, leads into the second character study: a Rhapsody, based on a sequence of three chords, with a hunting song and a postlude. This scene portrays Andres, unable to understand the mind of his friend Wozzeck, the interpreter of nature and, in spite of the human degradation to which he is subjected, a philosopher. The third scene, introduced by military music, presents Wozzeck's mistress, Marie, at first in a discussion, which degenerates into an argument, with her neighbour Margret (who reproaches her for her too friendly return of the Drum Major's greetings as he marches past), then alone with her boy (a Lullaby) and finally talking to Wozzeck, who, returning home for a moment, fantasizes about his impressions of nature and, after a few words, takes his leave. A passionate interlude leads into the fourth character study, that of the Doctor. He is represented by a Passacaglia, or rather a chaconne, the free recitative-like theme of which undergoes twenty-one variations brilliantly depicting the Doctor's *idée fixe* and his belief that Wozzeck is equally obsessed. In the fifth scene an *Andante Affettuoso* characterizes the Drum Major, to whose amorous advances Marie succumbs. With this scene ends the compressed exposition of the drama.

The second act, in which Wozzeck becomes aware of Marie's infidelity and is driven to despair by the torments and jeers of those around him, consists of a five-movement symphony. In the first scene Marie lulls her child to sleep and plays with the earrings which the Drum Major has given her. Wozzeck arrives and catches her doing this but Marie manages to soothe him. Musically the scene is a sonata first movement with exposition, first reprise, development, recapitulation and coda. In the second scene the Captain and the Doctor meet in the street (two fugue themes) and the former soon falls a victim to the Doctor's sadism. When Wozzeck later appears (a third theme), he becomes an object of ridicule to the two of them, who openly hint at Marie's unfaithfulness. This 'trialogue' finds its appropriate musical expression in the form of a Fantasy and Fugue on three themes. The closing section of the Fugue leads into a *Largo* for chamber orchestra (placed apart from the main orchestra), which then plays in the third scene. The main orchestra interjects only now and again in the scene to express the growing agitation of Wozzeck, who has a violent argument with Marie during which she brusquely admits her infidelity. The fourth scene is the setting for a splendid musical description of a milieu: the tavern life of the young lads, soldiers and girls: wine, song and dance present opportunities for a Ländler, a Waltz, duets, solos, a male-voice chorus and an amusing sermon by a young travelling apprentice. This sermon takes the form of a Melodrama which, accompanied by tavern music, parodies the chorale melody played on the bombardon. During this colourful scene, which forms the scherzo of the symphony, Wozzeck sees Marie dancing with the Drum Major and the thought of revenge gradually grows stronger in his poor incensed soul. The development of the Scherzo leads into the fifth scene, a Rondo marziale which describes the Drum Major, who, drunk and full of himself after his conquest, comes crashing into the guard-room and adds mockery to affliction by jeering at Wozzeck and beating him until he bleeds, thus completing his mental breakdown.

The third act, which in a short and dramatic conclusion shows the murder of Marie and Wozzeck's subsequent desperation and suicide, consists of six inventions each of which is based on one particular unifying musical idea. The third act pays the term 'invention' the highest honour. The first scene, an invention on a theme, with seven variations and a fugue, shows us Marie with her child as, repenting too late, she searches the Bible for comfort and forgiveness. The fifth of these variations, with its ballad-like melody, is one of the most enchanting parts of the opera. The closing section of the fugue leads into the second scene, in which Wozzeck and Marie meet for the last time. The meeting brings their last kiss – but also Marie's last hour. The music, tender and heartfelt during their last kiss, rises at the moment of murder to the highest dramatic expression, only to die away again rapidly and close with a pedal point on the note B♮, which has dominated the entire scene (the scene was an invention on a single note) and which now, as a transition to the third scene, forms a crescendo from *ppp* to *fff* in the whole orchestra (without drums). After this a rhythmic theme is played on the solo bass drum, a theme that looks simply bizarre but that gains in importance in the third scene (an invention on a rhythm), in which it is constantly employed, albeit with the most varied augmentation and diminution of the note-values and with constant changes in the harmony and melody. This idea or invention is surely unique in music: I at least have not yet found anything similar in music literature. This rhythmic theme in fact represents the tortured conscience of Wozzeck, who in this scene tries to drown his sorrow with drink and with prostitutes. The popular melody which is played on the out-of-tune pub piano during the singing and dancing is based on this rhythmic theme, as is also Wozzeck's drinking song, the song of the prostitute and the ensemble of the drinkers, who discover the blood marks on Wozzeck's arm and, in a threatening chorus, question him until he takes flight. Throughout the development-like transition to the fourth scene the rhythmic idea is emphasized, in various note values and beginning on different points of entry, in every orchestral part. In the fourth scene, Wozzeck's suicide scene, the invention uses a six-note chord (A♯, C♯, E, G♯, D♯, F) as the unifying idea, employing it at first as a chord which is split up in various ways and forms different melodies and then at different transpositions until it finally appears as chromatic sequences, symbolizing the movement of the water in which Wozzeck has found redemption. The croaking of the toads in this scene is derived from the same chord and, because of its accurate imitation of nature, creates a unique musical effect. The fifth invention in D minor (and thus an invention on a key) forms the orchestral interlude before the last scene. In this epilogue Wozzeck's tragic story is retold as a grandiose lament. There follows the fifth scene in which the children who are playing invite Marie's child to look at the body of his mother by the pond. Here the invention is based on a continuous, toccata-like quaver rhythm, a significant choice for something that will form the basis of the saddest scene, in which the sight of the innocent orphaned child arouses a deep melancholy in the sympathetic soul and the hope that fate will be kinder to him than it has been to his parents.

The reader will now understand that so diverse an opera is, in its architectonic structure, something that has really been created 'for the first time'. But the idea behind the form of this work is not the most telling factor nor is it an end in itself. It is just one of the work's merits. If space allowed me to describe all the other admirable parts of the piece which gave me such pleasure when I was working on the vocal score I should, to do Berg justice, have to describe all the striking instrumental ideas, the elegance and the nobility of the musical language, the refinement of a spirit which admits no clichés, the unique personal style and the innumerable musical treasures that pour forth from the creative cornucopia of this master of sound. As it is, these few words must suffice to express my conviction, a conviction based not on the subjective impression of a successful performance but on an objective knowledge of the work: that Berg's opera is, in the most comprehensive and exalted sense of the word, music, music and again music.

Musikblätter des Anbruch, 15 (1923), pp. 216–19

5. Alban Berg's 'Wozzeck':

A contribution to the problem of opera
by Ernst Viebig, Berlin

One feels almost ashamed when faced with the courage of this composer, who dares to put his ideas so rigorously into action at the obvious risk of being ridiculed by his contemporaries. Here really is someone for whom there are no compromises.

Far be it from me to attempt a 'critique'. In order to do that I would have to penetrate deeper into the work than is possible with the vocal score. When I first saw the score of Alban Berg's opera *Wozzeck* I was amazed at its technical difficulties in so far as playing it on the piano was concerned. Completely new technical accomplishments are necessary even to begin to play the piano part. The arranger, Fritz Heinrich Klein, had to devise some very complicated fingerings and playing methods to accommodate the enormous number of parts in a fairly practical way. In the full score Alban Berg used a system of special signs to indicate the principal and secondary parts and this same method (which is not new, incidentally, but was used by Arnold Schoenberg in his Five Orchestral Pieces, in *Erwartung* and in *Die glückliche Hand*) has been adopted in the vocal score. This makes the playing of it easier since one can see at a glance what is essential. What is also good, and worth copying, is that the pitch of the very low bass and the very high treble-clef notes, those needing some five or more ledger lines, is also indicated by a small letter. An impression of the orchestral sound has been recorded with the greatest care in the vocal score. The tremendous rhythmic liveliness of the music, although the individual rhythmic patterns often interlock and cancel one another, requires here and there that the separate beats are marked with numbers – a great help when studying. All in all the vocal score is a masterpiece and one cannot praise too highly the care and love lavished on it.

If I want now to talk about the opera itself I must first point out that the term 'opera' raises an almost impossible number of questions of the most difficult kind. The problem of 'opera' remains as unsolved today as it was in Mozart's time. Now, more than ever perhaps, Mozart's operas pose the most far-reaching stylistic questions. The more attempts are made to resolve these matters the more confusing they become.

Stylistically Alban Berg's *Wozzeck* stems directly from Franz

Schreker's *Der ferne Klang*, a work which has as special a position amongst Schreker's output as *Elektra* has amongst that of Strauss, since it was the inspiration for the thought-provoking, highly intellectual, modern opera. The twenty-five scenes in Georg Büchner's *Wozzeck* must have been very tempting for a modern composer to set to music, in spite of the difficulty of adapting them for the stage. After a thorough study of the text, Alban Berg came to the conclusion that it was possible so to transform Büchner's tragedy that it could, in spite of its sometimes overblunt and often brutal speech and action, be made suitable for operatic and stage treatment. The extent to which Berg used the different published versions and editions – Karl Emil Franzos, Paul Landau or Georg Witokowski – is not relevant here. It is enough that he managed – through alteration of scenes, some toning down and a relatively few omissions – first, to limit the number of characters, secondly, to reduce the plot to fifteen scenes and, thirdly, to refine the language to such an extent that it was possible to sing it. In connection with this third point it is necessary to investigate one characteristic of the work a little more deeply.

The 'rhythmic declamation' that had already been introduced by Arnold Schoenberg in *Pierrot lunaire* and *Erwartung*, is applied here in a way that has considerable operatic possibilities. And the composer goes even further than this in that he allows the voice to change from normal speech to rhythmic declamation, for example, and from there to the full singing voice. I can well imagine that, given a parallel spiritual and musical build-up, this kind of intensification could be most impressive.

Such things are superficial, however – external details on a par with the arrangement of the orchestra or the use of a separate chamber orchestra and a military and tavern band. The problems tackled by the work and which cast light on the whole problem of 'opera' lie deeper; it is in the *form* of the piece that the composer opens up new paths.

Richard M. Meyer captures the essential events of the tragedy in a few words: 'The hero is drawn from the common people, poor, weak and despised. Because of this he becomes a symbolic figure. He *is* the people and his fate is that of the people at the hands of those with power over them. To the Doctor he is only an experimental object; the fat Captain, who cries when he thinks of his own goodness, preaches morality to him. . .his lover, a defiant, sensual being, allows herself to be seduced by the Drum Major's animalistic splendour –

the seducer even mocks the poor cuckold. . .The way in which the derangement of Wozzeck's mind is portrayed is masterful: how the idea of murder takes root, how he withstands and then succumbs to it, and how the happy playing of the orphaned child is shaped into the shrill final chord.'

As I have already said, Alban Berg reduced the twenty-five scenes to fifteen, leaving him with three acts of five scenes each, with which, in an operatic sense, he could do something. The dramatic events are cleverly compressed, especialy in the way in which the first two acts generate great tension by finishing with external conflicts. In the last scene of the first act Wozzeck's mistress, Marie, surrenders to the Drum Major; in the last scene of the second act Wozzeck discovers the brutal truth. The third act only shows the inevitable consequence of these events: the murder of Marie – despair – suicide. Büchner's fractured sequence of events, the wild mixture of robust naturalism, philosophy and mysticism, with some scenes and moods that are wholly transcendental, must have meant that from the very conception of the piece one of the primary considerations was the question of musical form. *In this score absolute musical forms and the demands of the libretto find the perfect fusion.*

The first act contains 'Five character pieces', the exposition of the drama. Those people who bear the weight of the plot – 'the Captain', 'Andres', 'Marie', 'the Doctor' and finally 'the Drum Major' – are compared as characters to Wozzeck, the centre of all that happens. These five scenes show the enslaved Wozzeck in relation to his milieu. The lullaby of Marie, as she sings her little boy, Wozzeck's child, to sleep, is one of the most lyrical inspirations that I know of in any modern opera. (Act I scene 3, bar 363: see music supplement [provided with the original article]). But this rough structuring of the form is not enough. At the beginning of the work the composer gives a table which shows the complete formal structure of his opera. Within these five character pieces old formal designs, of a purely musical nature that has nothing to do with considerations about individual words, are being brought back to life. I shall content myself with naming only the most important of these smaller forms, although they themselves contain subdivisions and additions: Suite, Rhapsody, Military March, Passacaglia with 21 variations, *Andante Affettuoso.*

In order to clarify and illustrate the composer's achievement I would like to analyse the subdivisions of one of these pieces and have chosen the Suite, which consists of: Prelude, Sarabande,

Cadenza (viola), Gigue, Cadenza (double bassoon), Gavotte, Double I, Double II, Air, Reprise of the Prelude in retrograde, Finale (development). This is witness to both a fanatical impulse towards and an equally great knowledge of form.

The separate parts of the second act, a 'Symphony in five movements', consist of the following: a sonata-form first movement (of almost classical character), Fantasy and Fugue on three themes, *Largo* for chamber orchestra, Scherzo, Rondo. Thus the music here also is based on classical forms. The formal question was most difficult to deal with in the third act. Berg has achieved a natural solution by designing it as six inventions, the fifth of which is an orchestral interlude. Since he had to place the murder of Marie near the middle of the act there was the danger that, had he built the scene from the standpoint of this dramatic 'bombshell', the second part of the act, after the murder, might prove an anticlimax.

The text of the third act is so fine that the whole act has a slightly unworldly and unreal appearance. Because of the way in which the scenes are arranged, the first four of this act take place at night (in the first we have, within a few bars, Marie's remorse, her turning to God and her desperate spiritual turmoil); the fifth scene takes place in the cruel morning sunlight after the murder, the children playing with all the unconscious brutality that children possess. This act is like a night-time apparition – everything is more felt than real. All this is masterfully done! Six inventions – on a theme, on a note, a rhythm, a chord of six notes, a key and on a continuous quaver pattern.

The merging in this work of opera and absolute musical forms, which is quite new and is rigorously carried out, would be a step forward – perhaps even a *great* step forward – if the opera did not, at least as things are at present, hold within it its own demise. Perhaps it can be resurrected in the future, when more things are technically possible. But the work places such enormous demands on the singers and the orchestra that one would have to rehearse for at least a year in order to produce even a reasonably acceptable version.

Herr Alban Berg, you seem to be very optimistic about the technical and musical capabilities of singers. All your cast would need voices as wonderful as those heard at the 'Wintergarten' in Berlin. With average, or even above-average, singers your roles would be partly spoken and partly shrieked. What I'd like to call the 'over-contrapuntality' which sometimes – I say sometimes! – gives the impression that it is only there for the sake of the idea itself, to stay true to your school of thought but which doesn't always seem necessary, will make it almost impossible to stage a decent production. But half-measure would only confuse and damage the work.

Alban Berg's Op. 7 is, nevertheless, a *feat*; the rigorous carrying through of an idea that will stimulate and set new targets for opera production in our time. Perhaps the road to a truly 'musical opera' lies here – away from music drama.

Die Musik, 15 (1923), pp. 507–10

6. Creating atonal opera

by Emil Petschnig, Vienna

The April 1923 edition of *Musik* contained, amongst other things, an article from the pen of Ernst Viebig entitled 'Alban Berg's "Wozzeck" – a contribution to the problem of opera'. The contents of this article immediately made me want to get to know the work because, for many years, I have been greatly interested in the sphinx-like riddle of this particular art form and in the various modern attempts at finding a solution. I also hope to make some personal contribution to the regeneration of sung drama. I was even more intrigued by the article when I read that 'it is in the *form* of the piece that the composer opens up new paths', since that corresponds with my own opinion that the secret of a successful opera lies in its ability to accommodate the dramatic action within an architectonic musical structure. I was somewhat surprised therefore, especially today in these times of unlimited individuality, to discover that Berg's idea was to use the antiquated conventional forms of absolute music – such forms as the Suite, Passacaglia with variations, Sonata form, Fantasia and Fugue on three themes, Scherzo, Rondo, Invention on a theme, on one note, on a rhythm and so on – as the basis of the fifteen scenes of his dramatic work. I said to myself, however, that if the canon can be a means of dramatic expression, as it is in *Fidelio* and especially in *Onegin* (Lenski's and Onegin's duet before the duel), if the fugue and fugato have already shown that they can be effective on stage (*Meistersinger*, Prize song; *Carmen*, 1st finale), if the marches and dances of earlier times belong to the basic elements of this genre, why should it not for once be possible to find other ways of using the forms of absolute music?

In principle this method should leave itself open to the kind of mixing of styles that is so popular nowadays. With luck it should be possible to arrange the musical interpretation of psychological events, or arrange the dramatic situations to fit the motivic structure of a sonata or rondo movement in such a way that neither suffers – that the one does not lose the conciseness of its expression nor the other the clear differentiation of its formal structure.

Anxiously wondering how A. Berg would reconcile the differences between the freely developing tendencies of drama and the fixed, established formal shapes of pure music, I therefore opened the vocal score and searched (following Viebig's advice) for the Suite which provides the framework for the first scene. But apart from a few bars of chromatic passagework in 3/8 time (Vocal score pp. 15–18) which are supposed to represent the Gigue, a section in C about morality representing the Gavotte and its two Doubles (pp. 19–22) and a section in 3/2 to which, out of much good will, one might apply the term 'Air', I was unable to discover anything that resembled a Suite or even to discover any of those features that immediately differentiate the old dance forms from one another.

The second scene corresponds to the main characteristics of a rhapsody only to the extent that (like the soul of its hero gripped by his *idée fixe*) the music is very formless. The third scene pretends to be based on a military march, but this appears only at the beginning, when it serves to introduce the Drum Major (Wozzeck's later rival) to the public, after which it disappears without trace. The kind of structure that one has in the Finale of *Aida*, for example, is quite out of the question.

There follows, in scene 4, a Passacaglia with twenty-one variations. If the composer had not numbered every variation in order to make his intentions clear nobody would have recognized the movement as such from these monotonous sounds. And yet here, if anywhere, he could have used the shortness of the theme to take the opportunity to write music in which rapid changes mirrored the dramatic arguments for and against.

The fifth and last scene of the first act is meant to be an *Andante Affettuoso* which accompanies the Drum Major's wooing of Wozzeck's lover, Marie. The idea that a tempo indication can be a 'movement' leaves everything so open that even an opera scene can be included within this definition. One of the many love scenes from Mozart or Wagner could as easily, and with more justification, be cited as demonstrating the 'new'.

According to E. Viebig, 'The separate parts of the second act, a "Symphony in five movements", consist of the following: a sonata-form first movement (of almost classical character), Fantasy and Fugue on three themes, *Largo* for chamber orchestra, Scherzo, Rondo. Thus the music here also is based on classical forms.'

I must admit that I failed to reconstruct the Sonata from its thematic infusoria. The 'Fantasia' follows the atonalists' usual habit of aimlessly messing around in all twenty-four musical (or should I say non-musical?) keys and I should have thought that the motivic basis for the triple fugue would have been taken from the characteristics that have already been established for the three people involved in this scene, the Captain and the Doctor who opens Wozzeck's eyes to the unfaithfulness of his mistress. By bringing these themes together the piece could have been given a dramatic character. Perhaps A. Berg wanted to do something like this but, if he did, it never quite shows. In the *Largo*, Wozzeck accuses Marie of her infidelity with the Drum Major, an accusation she curtly rejects. The Scherzo consists of a Ländler and a Waltz played by accordion, bombardon, two fiddles, clarinet and guitar; the scene is a tavern garden full of young men and women. The situation (Wozzeck is forced to watch as Marie and the Drum Major dance together), and therefore the form, is similar to that in *Hans Heiling* except that Marschner makes his dance reflect the mountain troll's state of mind and thus achieves a thrilling effect, an effect which is totally lacking in the present case. Instead there is here an effect, similar to that in *Der Rosenkavalier*, of stage and orchestral music weaving in and out of one another. There are also several humorously intended moments reminiscent of the quintet of Jews in *Salome*. Nothing new there either.

The Rondo appears to be so called because the realistic snoring chorus of the soldiers sleeping in the barrack dormitories, which introduces the final scene, also separates the two dialogues of Wozzeck–Andres and Wozzeck–the Drum Major. This is certainly a high-handed interpretation of the term, as also has to be said for the 'Inventions' in the final act. The first invention consists of three attempts at an imitative working out of a melodic succession of fourths followed by the obligatory fugue. The second invention, on a single note (B♮), using many different registers and instrumentations, succeeds in so far as the ostinato strengthens the eerie atmosphere created by the orchestra (muted brass, low woodwind, muted and much divided strings, tam-tam and other percussion instruments), a picture of the woodland path by the pond where, under the rising blood-red moon, Wozzeck stabs the unfaithful mother of his child. Weber had already used this idea in his 'Wolf's Glen'. It is even less original to create a 'polyphony' by separating the atonal parts into high and low voices; even the incompatible can become compatible if one uses this method. The rhythm ♩ | ♪♪ | ♩. | ♫♪♪, which is repeated here and there in the third invention, derives from a quick polka on an out-of-tune piano. If I say that five or six, and often eight or nine, even eleven (from the bottom up B, F, G♯, A♯, C, D, A, C♯, E, G, B♭) chromatically adjacent notes are, quite regularly, all played together then you will have to believe me when I say that the whole opera sounds as if it were played on an out-of-tune piano.

The next invention, on a six note-chord (B♭, C♯, E, G♯, E♭, F; or B♭, C♯, D♯, E, F, A♭; or E, F, A♭, B♭, D♯, E and so on), also contributes to what can only be called this pathologically cacophonous ecstasy. The calls of the toads in this scene – Wozzeck tries to sink the knife, which is evidence of his crime, in the deepest part of the pond and drowns in the attempt – have been very realistically represented. An *adagio* orchestral interlude (which, by the way, links all the scenes of the act thematically) forms the fifth invention 'on a key', the only time that a key signature (one flat) appears next to a clef. Otherwise every – and I mean every – note of the vocal score has its own accompanying accidental, something which certainly does not make it easy to play fluently from the manuscript. Even so the tonality of the interlude is not up to much: already during the first few bars Berg moves away to barely related areas. After two pages the flat is completely cancelled (it apparently being unnecessary) so that the piece actually consists of two or four (it is hard to say whether major or minor) keys. This is, therefore, a harmonic farce and much of what has gone before resembles a formal bluff. The final scene with the children, which stands in great contrast to what has just gone before, is dominated by a continuous quaver movement with much rubato. It represents the last of the six inventions and contains nothing whatsoever to elicit anyone's admiration.

Ever since people started writing operas, certain distinct situations have been represented by certain characteristic rhythms, emotive themes, timbres. It is true that this dramatic technique has been neglected over the last few decades, as German composers have fallen under the spell of Wagner's 'unending melody'; nor can one deny the complete decline in sung drama of the vocal forms which belonged to this earlier principle. But Alban Berg is far from putting forward this problem for discussion in its essential form. He deceives himself and others when he claims with this work to have done anything more than simply raise the question yet again. At the very best one can only speak of feeble attempts at recreating opera through certain formal devices but these attempts drown hopelessly in a jumble of chords and voices. A musico-dramatic renaissance demands far more resolute action, a complete break with the present trend as represented by Strauss or even by Schreker, a wholly new alignment and a completely fresh start; steps similar to those that have already been taken in instrumental music by moving away from the gigantic, massive symphony to the intimacy of chamber music.

Wozzeck lends itself to extremely realistic treatment, but its subject and its prose are quite unsuitable for setting to music in a style which, after the maid has acted the mistress and the orchestra dominated the scene for so long, must take singing as its starting point. But what our present composer expects of a voice defies description and indicates total unfamiliarity with the subject. Even E. Viebig cannot conceal this in his final paragraph. The vocal parts in *Wozzeck* spell certain ruin for the singer, who, at some points, has to sing in horrendously high registers and who does not even have a melody but must sing in *Sprechgesang* and then rhythmically declaim this *Sprechgesang* in the manner of Schoenberg's *Pierrot* melodramas, in which the note value has to be held exactly and the pitch approximately. This is a completely unnatural method and – with the voice being required to cover over two octaves – borders on caricature, since it is well-known that the inflexion of our speech, even at moments of great emotion, moves only within an octave. And finally the singer has also to speak normally. It is not enough that the performer has to pitch his voice throughout against the excessive over-contrapuntality and the correspondingly massive orchestration; he must also constantly readjust his method of delivery. This is something behind which I could see absolutely no inner necessity or even any consistent principle such as, for example, the desire for intensification – the wish to progress from the spoken through recitative and melodrama to song, or the distinguishing of what is real from what is ideal, in the way that a writer like Shakespeare does so brilliantly through his use of prose and verse.

The vocal range of everyday speech is often accurately recorded in the notes of the opera (Act I scenes 1, 4 and 5, Act II scenes 2 and 3), but the purpose of music, surely, is to lift the word out of these troughs, to take it above the sphere of rhythmic poetic language and back to its starting point in the primal world of melody.

But, as I have said, there is little of this to be found here and those sections in which some kind of melody could not be avoided, sections such as the Military March, the Ländler and Waltz, the hunting song and the verse 'Ins Schwabenland da mag ich nit. . .', display a poverty of imagination that tries in vain to hide itself behind the most complicated and twisted harmony, harmony that does not suit the nature of these traditional pieces. There is a lack of stylistic sense and of talent for characterization – the main requirements of a dramatist! – here from which the rest of the piece also suffers more than a little. The score, which reveals so hypertrophic an enlargement of parts and chords that it sometimes needs four hands to play it, would lend itself to a subtle musico-psychological interpretation of a quite exceptionally complicated kind; what we are really dealing with here, however, are quite simple people who naively abandon themselves to their sexual instincts, and there is therefore an incongruence, a lack of truth about the way in which things are expressed, which is that much greater because of the lack of individual motives and the constant to and fro, backwards and forwards of phrases and figures instead of big, simple, flowing lines which would bring out the spiritual content of the scene. A. Berg showers both the important and the insignificant, the most distressing as well as the most trivial (one need only look at the accompaniment to the Doctor's words in Act I scene 4: 'Have you eaten your beans yet, Wozzeck? Nothing but beans, nothing but legumes! Mark my words! Next week we'll start with mutton!' etc.) with the same deluge of sounds so that any structuring, any distribution of light and shade or foreground and background which might help the vividness of the drama is impossible. No doubt there are in the details quite a few fine touches that show a keen observation of reality – especially in Act II scene 2 – and the score itself looks very impressive and often raises expectations of a music in line with the events on stage. But when played it becomes an unimaginative, shapeless and slow clutter of dissonances which, because it lacks variety, rapidly becomes dull. Music should be taken in not only with the eye but with the ear, the highest court of judgment.

One cannot deny that our author has a certain feeling for powerful, theatrically effective moments; it was a feeling that led him to choose Büchner's fragment, the social tendencies of which might even have added unusual colour to the vague romanticism, mysticism and symbolism of present-day opera. But instead of this earthy subject being shaped with a few rough strokes, leaving out everything that is episodic or takes up excessive room, the thing has been blown up into a long, large-scale affair that does nothing to show that the 'perfect fusion of absolute musical forms with the demands of the libretto', which E. Viebig claims and praises as the new musico-dramatic revelation, is a fact or even that it is a possibility. I continue to entertain the greatest scepticism about this, believing that one should give to each – absolute as well as dramatic music – its own. Only in Germany, in a nation whose dramatic instinct is so underveloped that it refuses to recognize its own theatrical geniuses, that it forced Gluck to realize his ideas about artistic reform on foreign soil, thought little of Mozart, Weber, Lortzing and mocked Wagner throughout his life, placing (out of envy and indolence) many obstacles in the way of his efforts to create a national music drama – and this is not even to mention Kleist, Grabbe and Hebbel! – only in a nation which obtains (in fact, must obtain) most of its theatrical repertoire from France and Italy, could such aesthetic confusion, such a jumble of theories arise, receive acclaim and even material support. And at the same time, the true opera composer still has to stand aside and watch how such experiments waste years during which, had the mentality of those who are influential in the theatre been different, we could have enjoyed a revival of national music drama that was both artistically and financially rewarding.

There are many things left to discuss, but I have confined myself to the most essential. It seems to me to be my duty to express these things and to point out the unsoundness and the drawbacks of the system which *Wozzeck* attempts to use. I only feel regret at the undoubtedly considerable knowledge of compositional technique that has been used on this, in itself inconsistent, exercise.

Die Musik, 16/5 (February 1924), pp. 340–5

7. The musical forms in my opera 'Wozzeck'

by Alban Berg, Vienna

Far be it from me to oppose the musico-theoretical views of Herr Emil Petschnig – every bar of my music does that better than words ever could – but I would like to correct a few of the vast number of obvious untruths in his article 'Creating atonal opera'. It is not true that the second scene of the first act 'corresponds to the main characteristics of a Rhapsody only in that its music is very formless'. On the contrary, it is, since it is based on a succession of three chords upon the free variation of which is built the development of the entire scene, a completely closed form the clear shape of which was also made apparent by the fact that three verses and the refrain of a hunting song (written in a folk-like style, in accordance with the true characteristics of a rhapsody) are placed at carefully considered points of the structure. Similarly, the 'Fantasia' of the second scene of Act II by no means 'follows the atonalists' usual habit of messing around' but – fulfilling the point of combining a 'fantasy and fugue' – prepares for the following triple fugue, in this case by, amongst other things, introducing and assimilating its themes in a planned way (on a more harmonic basis at first) and thus striving towards the pure contrapuntal form of the fugue which is its true objective. Herr Petschnig's further criticism, that he would 'have thought that the motivic basis for the triple fugue would have been taken from the characteristics that have already been established for the three people involved in this scene' thus becomes redundant, especially so if I tell him that these three themes have, in fact, been taken from earlier scenes that established these characteristics. Similarly, his confession that he failed 'to reconstruct the Sonata from its thematic infusoria' is by no means a proof that its form is not in accordance with that of a strict classical movement (with exposition, varied reprise, development and recapitulation with coda) of which the first subject, transition, second subject and closing sections are clearly recognizable as such and are, as far as their scope is concerned, no more 'infused' than are those of many of Beethoven's sonatas. The further assertion that 'the Scherzo (of Act II scene 4) consists of a Ländler and a Waltz' describes the form of the scene inadequately (because it has been misunderstood) and thereby denies its construction as a symphonic movement. The truth is that these two dances are only part of a symmetrically built movement following classical models, namely: Scherzo I, Trio I, Scherzo II – Trio II – Scherzo I, Trio I, Scherzo II. Once this correction is made all tendentious references to *Hans Heiling*, *Rosenkavalier* and *Salome* become completely uncalled for. I have, on the other hand, to agree with Herr Petschnig that it is 'certainly a high-handed interpretation of the term' to call one section a Rondo, as he has done. It is in fact only the introduction to such. The 'Rondo marziale' (Act II scene 5), which in terms of its form and character has been handled very strictly, really begins just at the point at which Herr Petschnig has stopped his analysis. A similar method of criticizing by distorting the truth proves equally worthwhile in his discussion of the *adagio* orchestral interlude in the last act (Act III scenes 4–5). Not recognizing that we are in this case quite clearly dealing with a three-part structure in D minor, he complains that 'the tonality of this interlude is not up to much' and that the key signature 'is completely cancelled (it apparently being unnecessary)'. But what in fact happens is that the middle section (which Bussler calls the 'modulating section') which follows this cancellation leads back to the main key, in which the piece now continues and in which the *adagio* finishes as clearly as it began; this is made clear by the reintroduction of key signatures, thus visibly refuting Herr Petschnig's claim that 'the piece actually consists of two or even four (it's hard to say whether major or minor) keys. This is therefore a harmonic farce and much of what has gone before resembles a formal bluff.' Thank God that it is only a resemblance! Which is to say that proof, even if successful in the case of the farce, cannot be so easily produced in the case of the bluff, despite the resemblance! Let us take the invention on a rhythm of the third scene of Act III as an example. If the formal principle behind it was merely that a certain rhythm was repeated 'here and there' in it, then it really would not be entitled to being rated as a formal principle. In fact, however, the whole piece is built on this one rhythm which serves, at the same time, as its theme. Subjected to every conceivable combination, contrapuntal device (fugato, stretti) and variation (augmentation, diminution, displacement etc.), this one rhythm permeates all the harmonic, thematic and vocal events in the scene. To recognize this – and much else as well – should not be difficult. Of course, one needs, besides good will, a certain degree of competence – a competence that seems in this case to be lacking in musical and in other areas. Büchner's work could not otherwise have been misunderstood to the extent that the comment that 'what we are really dealing with here are quite simple people who naively abandon themselves to their sexual instincts' reveals. This makes all the more astonishing the accurate judgment that the treatment of the *Sprechgesang* in the tavern scene of Act II is a 'completely unnatural method and borders on caricature'. For that is precisely what it is: a completely drunk travelling apprentice delivering a sermon on fasting. It is a caricature in the truest sense of the word, as is also revealed in its musical setting (something that, like much else, is not mentioned): a chorale melody on the bombardon against which the other instruments provide a counterpoint of tavern music in the form of a strict four-voiced chorale prelude.

One can believe me when I say that these and other musical forms are successful at the points at which they were intended to be; and also that I am capable of proving their correctness and legitimacy in a more thorough, and thus a more conclusive, manner than has been possible here.

Anyone who wishes to be convinced of this should get in touch with me; I shall be happy to oblige.

Die Musik, 16 (1924), pp. 587–9

8. A word about 'Wozzeck'

by Alban Berg

It is now ten years since I started to compose *Wozzeck*; already so much has been written about it that I can hardly say anything without plagiarizing my critics. I should like, however, to correct an error that arose in 1925 soon after it was produced and that has spread widely since.

I have never entertained the idea of reforming the structure of opera through *Wozzeck*. Neither when I started nor when I completed the work did I consider it a model for further efforts by any other composer. I never assumed or expected that *Wozzeck* should become the basis of a school.

I simply wanted to compose good music; to develop musically the contents of Georg Büchner's immortal drama; to translate his poetic language into music. Other than that, when I decided to write an opera, my only intention, as related to the technique of composition, was to give the theatre what belongs to the theatre. The music was to be so formed that at each moment it would fulfil its duty of serving the action. Even more, the music should be prepared to furnish whatever the action needed for transformation into reality on the stage. The function of a composer is to solve the problems of an ideal stage director. On the other hand this objective should not prejudice the development of the music as an entity, absolute, and purely musical. No externals should interfere with its individual existence.

That I accomplished these purposes by a use of musical forms more or less ancient (considered by critics as one of the most important of my ostensible reforms of the opera) was a natural consequence of my method. It was first necessary to make a selection from Büchner's twenty-five loosely constructed, partly fragmentary scenes for the libretto. Repetitions not lending themselves to musical variation were avoided. Finally, the scenes were brought together, arranged, and grouped in acts. The problem therefore became more musical than literary, and had to be solved by the laws of musical structure rather than by the rules of dramaturgy.

It was impossible to shape the fifteen scenes I selected in different manners so that each would retain its musical coherence and individuality and at the same time follow the customary method of development appropriate to the literary content. No matter how rich structurally, no matter how aptly it might fit the dramatic events, after a number of scenes so composed the music would inevitably create monotony. The effect would become boring with a series of a dozen or more formally composed entr'actes which offered nothing but this type of illustrative music, and boredom, of course, is the last thing one should experience in the theatre.

I obeyed the necessity of giving each scene and each accompanying piece of entr'acte music – prelude, postlude, connecting link or interlude – an unmistakable aspect, a rounded off and finished character. It was imperative to use everything essential for the creation of individualizing characteristics on the one hand, and coherence on the other. Hence the much discussed utilization of both old and new musical forms and their application in an absolute music.

The appearance of these forms in opera was to some degree unusual, even new. Nevertheless novelty, pathbreaking, was not my conscious intention. I must reject the claim of being a reformer of the opera through such innovations, although I do not wish to depreciate my work thereby, since others who do not know it so well can do that much better.

What I do consider my particular accomplishment is this. No one in the audience, no matter how aware he may be of the musical forms contained in the framework of the opera, of the precision and logic with which it has been worked out, no one, from the moment the curtain parts until it closes for the last time, pays any attention to the various fugues, inventions, suites, sonata movements, variations, and passacaglias about which so much has been written. No one gives heed to anything but the vast social implications of the work which by far transcend the personal destiny of Wozzeck. This, I believe, is my achievement.

Modern Music, (November–December 1927), pp. 22ff

9. A lecture on 'Wozzeck'

by Alban Berg

[Most references to the vocal score represent excerpts from *Wozzeck* performed in the course of the lecture.]

When, fifteen years ago, I decided to compose the opera *Wozzeck*, the musical situation was very unusual. We of the Viennese school, under the leadership of Arnold Schoenberg, had just developed beyond the beginnings of the movement that people quite wrongly called atonality. At first composition in that style was restricted to the creation of small forms such as songs, piano pieces and orchestral pieces or, if it was a question of extended works (such as the twenty-one *Pierrot* melodramas of Schoenberg or his two, one-act, stage works), to forms that, without exception, derived their shape from a text or a dramatic basis. The so-called atonal style still lacked large-scale works – works with a traditional four-movement structure and of a size that had until then been usual, symphonies, oratorios, large operas. And the reason for this was that in renouncing tonality the style renounced with it one of the strongest and best-proved means of building small- and large-scale formal structures.

Once I had decided to write an opera that would last a whole evening I faced a new problem, at least as far as harmony was concerned: how, without the proven means of tonality and without being able to use the formal structures based on it, could I achieve the same sense of completeness, the same compelling musical unity? And, what is more, a sense of self-containedness not only in the small-scale structure of the scenes themselves (I shall have a lot to say about this later) but also, what was much more difficult, a sense of completeness in the larger structures of the single acts and, indeed, in the architecture of the work as a whole?

Text and action alone could not guarantee this unity; certainly not in a work like Büchner's *Wozzeck* which, as is well known, consists of many (twenty-three) loose, fragmentary scenes. And even if it were possible to find a three-act scheme which achieved some unity of dramatic action, by arranging the scenes in three groups of five in a way that clearly distinguished between exposition, peripetia and catastrophe – so that a sense of dramatic unity was imposed on the work – this, in itself, would not give a sense of unity and completeness to the music.

We shall see in the course of my talk the different ways in which I have tried to achieve this. But first of all I would like to draw your attention to a harmonic feature and especially to the harmony at the end of each act. The point in a tonal composition at which the return to and establishment of the main key is made clear, so that it is recognizable to the eyes and ears of even the layman, must also be the point at which the harmonic circle closes in an atonal work.

This sense of closure was first of all ensured by having each act of the opera steer towards one and the same closing chord, a chord that acted in the manner of a cadence and that was dwelled on as if on a tonic.

At the end of Act I this chord is heard in the following form: [*Vocal score p. 81, bar 715 to end of act*]. At the end of Act II: [*Vocal score p. 180, bar 809 to end of act*]. At the end of Act III: [*Vocal score p. 231, bar 398 to end of act*].

You will notice – and it will strike you even more clearly when you hear it on the orchestra – that these closing chords, although always built from the same notes, always appear in a different form. These musical differences were not only determined by the changing situations resulting from the dramatic action. The desire for musical unity and (to use a term of Schoenberg's) musical coherence stands, of course, in opposition to another equally strong aspiration, which is the desire for musical variety, for a diversity of patterns. Thus Acts I and III close with the notes of the chord played simultaneously – I repeat: Act I: [*Vocal score p. 81, last bar*]; Act III: [*Vocal score p. 231, last bar*]. At the end of Act II, on the other hand, the chord dissolves, as it were, more and more into its constituent parts [*Vocal score p. 180, bar 809 to end*], leaving behind as its last vestige this low B♮.

I should like at this point to mention, in anticipation, that the low B that accompanies the prophetic last words of Act II ('He bleeds', 'One thing after another') has both dramatic significance and significance as regards the formal design for one of the most important of the later scenes. We shall come back to this point.

In order to show you even more clearly how this sense of, on the one hand, unity and, on the other, variety manifests itself I shall, in a moment, ask the orchestra to play the last scenes of the three acts. I should also like to say something about the formal effect of the way in which this important harmony links up to the beginning of the acts.

The dramatic content of the last scene of Act I is, put briefly, the seduction of Marie by the Drum Major; musically it is a rondo-like *Andante affettuoso* [*Vocal score: Act I, p. 73, bar 656 to end*]. The fairly short orchestral introduction to the following act, played while the curtain is still down, takes up this closing chord: [*Vocal score: Act II, p. 82, bars 1–6 (without the last quaver)*]. Then the curtain rises on Act II.

The last scene of Act II depicts the encounter between the jealous Wozzeck and the Drum Major, which ends with the defeat of Wozzeck. Notice, by the way, that the fight between the two in this scene is musically just the same as that between the Drum Major and Marie, which ended in her seduction, in the previous closing scene. Another means, therefore, of establishing a musical cohesion!

These and other dramatic parallels between the two closing scenes also bring about – quite unconsciously – a musical parallel. But whilst in the passionate *Andante* of the earlier scene the Rondo form is only hinted at, here the piece is structured, with true military precision, according to the strict formal rules of a Rondo, a real 'Rondo marziale' to be sure [*Vocal score: Act II, p. 173, bar 761 to end*].

The closing scene of Act III, and thus of the whole opera, is based on constant quavers, a sort of *perpetuum mobile* movement, which depicts the games and the play of the poor working-class children amongst whom is the completely unsuspecting child of Marie and Wozzeck, now orphaned twice over [*Vocal score: Act III, p. 229, bar 372 and previous upbeat to end*]. And thus the opera ends. And yet, although it again clearly moves to cadence on to the closing chord, it almost appears as if it carries on. And it does carry on! In fact, the opening bar of the opera could link up with this final bar and in so doing close the whole circle [*Vocal score: Act III, p. 231, last bar & Act I, p. 9, bars 1–3*].

This, like much else that I am now telling you, was not intentional and the theory behind it only became clear to me when I looked back on it ten or more years later. Thus, for example – to stay with this opening passage – there are two introductory string chords before the drama begins. In order to make the crescendo between the first and second chord clear there is a soft crescendo roll on the side drum. That was a purely instrumental, and thus a musical-acoustical, matter. But when I heard it for the first time I discovered, to my great astonishment, that I could not have indicated the military milieu of the piece in a more pregnant, more concise way than through this little side-drum roll.

To return to my attempts to have both a great variety and integration: from the different kinds of openings and closings of all three acts you have seen that there is enormous diversity in addition to the ways which the chord changes which we have already mentioned. In the first scene the curtain rises immediately after the first orchestral bar; at the end of the act it falls with the last bars of the music. The curtain at the beginning of the second act rises after the short orchestral introduction that you have already heard. When the music of this act has finished, the last stage picture is held for a moment and then the curtain falls. Similarly (again in an attempt to establish a connection) the curtain to Act III rises before the music begins. The music first starts after a (silent) pause. The final curtain eventually falls before the music has finished – not, as it did in the first act, to a chord that gradually increases in volume but before the unchanging pianissimo of the chord fades away.

Finally, in discussing these attempts to fashion a closed structure, to say something about the large-scale architecture of the opera: the methods by which I constructed the three acts of the work allow the whole piece to be interpreted as a traditional three-part (ABA) structure in so far as the first and third acts have certain architectural similarities (although, of course, the last act is not a musical reprise of the first). Of shorter playing time than Act II, the two outer acts enclose the much longer and weightier central act in what I should like to call a symmetry of time. And while, as we shall see, this central act exhibits from the first to last bars a totally integrated structure, the forms of the two outer acts are much freer. They consist of five loosely-connected pieces of music corresponding to the five loosely-related scenes of the act. The five scenes of Act I could be described as five character pieces each of which presents a new figure in the drama in relation to the main title figure – his superior officer the Captain, his friend Andres, his mistress Marie, the Doctor and the Drum Major. The five scenes of Act III consist of five musical forms the self-containedness of which is based on another principle of musical unity – the unity of a theme that is then varied, of a single note, a chord, a rhythm or a constant pattern of movement.

Thus, these two outer more loosely-structured acts, in which the scenes are concerned with a unifying idea (the five character pieces of the first act, the five unifying principles of the third) like the two 'A's of a three-part song form, enclose the more rigorously-structured central act, in which the five scenes are inseparably linked together as the movements of a (in this case, dramatic) symphony. That is, there is a sonata-form first movement followed by a Fantasia and Fugue on three themes, a slow movement (the *Largo*), a Scherzo and, finally, the 'Rondo marziale con introduzione' that we have already mentioned. The middle act, like the 'B' section of the corresponding three-part form, is thus clearly identified as the central part and is essentially different from the two 'A' sections, which are similar to one another in structure.

This discussion of some of the harmonic and formal features of the opera should be enough to make you aware of the large-scale cohesion of its music, a cohesion which, as I said at the beginning, was achieved without using tonality and the formal possibilities which spring from it.

Such cohesion was, of course, also necessary on a small scale and it may be that it was this simple consideration that led to the use of certain 'old forms', a use that has been much discussed and which until now has done as much as the performances to make the opera well known. In trying to achieve musical variety, and in order that a piece with so many scenes should not be totally 'durchkomponiert', as most music dramas since Wagner have been, there was nothing left but for me to find another shape for these fifteen scenes. On the other hand, the self-contained nature of these scenes required a self-containedness in the music, which in turn necessitated securing some kind of cohesion between these shapes and, in a word, giving each a closed musical structure. The dramatic application of these forms then resulted as naturally as the selection for this purpose of the forms themselves.

There was not, therefore, any desire for the 'archaic' in using such forms as variations, or even passacaglia and fugues in this opera and it would be even more wrong to suppose that these things had anything to do with the atavistic 'Back to. . .' movement, which, by the way, started much later. As a matter of fact to do what I needed I not only had to find these more or less 'old forms' but, as I have already shown in my short analysis of the three acts, I had to seize on new forms, or forms based on new principles such as those based on 'a note', 'a rhythm' or 'a chord'.

The relatively large number of musical interludes between scenes, resulting from the three scene changes that take place within the course of each act, was further reason for me to be as diverse and varied as possible. To have written symphonic transitions or intermezzi for all of these transitions (as I saw done later in the case of another contemporary work with a lot of scene changes) would not have accorded with my idea of music drama which, in spite of my respect for absolute music, I have never lost when composing for the theatre.

I was here also, therefore, forced to strive for a variety and contrast, making some of the interludes transitional, making some of them codas to the previous scene, some introductions to the following scene or in some cases combining these two functions. In doing this I sometimes tried to achieve an almost unnoticeable connection between the different parts of the musical forms while, elsewhere, I preferred abrupt juxtapositions. We shall hear some examples of these in the course of my talk.

I shall now go through the single scenes of the opera, less to guide you through all the musical forms (which, as I have said, the newspapers and specialist periodicals which have carried reviews of the piece have been providing for a long time now) but rather to take the opportunity, from time to time, to point out something that is not immediately obvious about the formal structure. Such as, for example, that the very first scene of the opera is designed as a suite may be due to the fact that the dialogue of this scene, in which nothing really takes place, is also made up from different loosely juxtaposed topics. It was natural to try to match these different topics with small musical forms which would together create a larger form, such as a suite, made up of a succession of such small musical units. That it proved to be a suite built mostly of old, and more or less stylized, forms – such as Prelude, Pavane, Cadenza, Gigue, Gavotte with Doubles – was no accident, even though it happened unconsciously. Through this the first scene acquires (albeit, as I said, unintentionally) what I would like to call a certain historical colouring. Listen, for example, to the Gigue of this Suite and then to a cadenza-like solo on the double bassoon which links the Gigue to the beginning of the Gavotte: [*Vocal score: Act I, pp. 15–19, bars 65–120 (first crotchet)*].

The feeling that the Suite has a completeness and self-containedness is achieved, amongst other things, through the little introductory Prelude returning like a refrain at the end of the scene, albeit in retrograde, which is to say that it runs note-for-note backwards. In this the music matches the example of the dramatic structure of the scene, in which topics from the opening also return at the end.

The first orchestral interlude, which follows the scene as a postlude, is simply a development of the main musical ideas of the different movements of the Suite.

Whereas the first scene is built on an old musical form, the scene that follows has a quite different basis. The unifying principle of this scene is harmonic: three chords which represent the harmonic skeleton of the scene [*Vocal score: Act I, p. 30, bars 203–4*]. That such a principle can act as a structural element will be admitted by anyone who thinks of tonality as a means of building forms and regards these three chords as having functions comparable to those of the tonic, dominant and subdominant. It goes without saying that the ways in which these chords and the chord sequence are presented are very diverse and varied throughout. To give one example: [*Vocal score: Act I, p. 30, bars 201–7* or *Vocal score: Act I, p. 32, bars 225 (or 227) to 234*].

I did not, of course, shun the chance of writing ariosos and song-like pieces. In fact, as examples, there are two songs in this scene and the next. The first of these, inserted between the presentations of the more rhapsodic chord pattern, is the three-strophe coloratura song of Andres. The following scene includes a military march and Marie's lullaby.

I should like to make two general observations at this point. The first concerns the handling of the singing voice in this opera. It has often been said that this is not a *bel canto* opera. But it is not often realized how much of what is regarded as truly vocal can also be achieved through a 'bel cantare' delivery. As I have said, I have never renounced the possibility of coloratura singing and indeed there is almost no recitative to be found in my opera. But I think that I have made ample amends for this deficiency by employing, for the first time and for a length of time that is unique in opera, the so-called 'rhythmic declamation' that Schoenberg introduced twenty years ago in the speaking chorus of *Die glückliche Hand* and in his *Pierrot* melodramas. It has proved that this 'melodramatic' method of handling the voice – while, it should be noted, fully preserving all the formal possibilities of absolute music in a way that recitative, for example, does not – that this melodically, dynamically and rhythmically determined way of speaking not only offers one of the best means of ensuring that the words are understood (as they must be from time to time in an opera); it has also enriched opera with a valuable means of expression, created from the purest musical sources, which – ranging from the pitchless whispered word to the true *bel parlare* of broad speech melodies – offers a welcome addition and an attractive contrast to the sung word.

My second observation concerns the way I have handled the folksongs in the work and the need to establish a relationship between art music and folk music, something that is fairly self-evident in tonal music. It was not easy to make these different levels clear in so-called atonal harmony. I think that I have been successful and I took great care to ensure that everything to do with folk music in the opera (including the atonal harmonies) has an easily understood simplicity. Thus, for example, these sections favour symmetrically built periods and phrase structures, harmonies that are based on thirds (or, more especially, fourths), and melodic patterns in which an important role is played by the whole tone scale and the perfect fourth, as opposed to the diminished and augmented intervals which otherwise dominate the atonal music of the Viennese school.

So called 'polytonality' is another such means of creating a harmonically primitive music. We find such a popular touch in the military march (with its 'false bass') and in Marie's lullaby with its fourth harmonies, pieces which the orchestra will now play to you. But, please, also notice during this performance the way in which the link with the second scene, about which I have already spoken, is effected. I have shown you the three chords of this second scene: [*Vocal score: Act I, p. 38, bar 286 (L.H. stronger)*]. The following three thirds in the bass are the basis of these chords: [*Vocal score, p. 38, bar 286 (first two crotchets)*]. From these spring the representation of the uncanny sunset with the following, more motivic, shape: [*Vocal score: Act I, p. 39, bars 286–93 (first crotchet)*]. Elsewhere these three chords become the harmonic basis of a wide-ranging melody: [*Vocal score: Act I, p. 39, bars 302–10 (or 312)*], which, leading to the end of this second rhapsodic scene, becomes the interlude music and leads in turn into the march of the approaching military band with which the next scene begins and which is then interrupted by the following song from Marie: [*Vocal score: Act I, pp. 38–48, bars 286–426*].

I have let the music be played up to this point and am only interrupting now in order to mention another dramatic device the only purpose of which, again, is to ensure a musical unity. These fifths [*Vocal score: Act I, p. 48, bars 425–6*] are, along with other recurring motives and musical shapes, characteristic of the figure of Marie. I could say that this point of harmonic repose depicts that aimless waiting, a waiting which finds its resolution only in her death. This idea is used several times, in the manner of a leitmotive. Similar repetitions are also found, as I have said, in the case of other motives that are associated with different characters and different situations.

I need hardly say that I have also exploited the possibilities of using these leitmotives, or rather motives of reminiscence, to establish connections and relationships and, therefore, as a further means of attaining unity. Let us take as an example the chords in the second scene which, one could say, are to be understood as a sound of nature. Here, in the second scene, they represent the inanimate nature which so terrifies Wozzeck; in the last scene of the second act they represent the nature sounds of the snores of the soldiers sleeping in the barracks. Here they appear on the orchestra; there in the form of a wordless chorus (sung with closed lips) which joins with the sound of Wozzeck groaning in his sleep: [*Vocal score: Act II, p. 169, bars 737–43*].

The Passacaglia or Chaconne of the fourth scene is built upon a twelve-note theme: [*Vocal score: Act I, p. 55, bars 486–7*].

Needless to say, the working out of the variations of this theme is not mechanical or even done in terms of pure, absolute music but has the strongest possible connection to the dramatic action. Even the first statement of the twelve-note row has a dramatic basis in that it appears with the first words of the scene, growing out of the speech of the Doctor and almost submerged by the excitement of the rubato of the 'cello recitative: [*Vocal score: Act I, pp. 55–6, bars 488–95*]. There then follow twenty-one variations: [*Vocal score: Act I, pp. 57–72, bars 496–642*]. These are true variations, concerned with one and the same theme, with the same *idée fixe* of the Doctor, an *idée fixe* which finds its echo when the harrassed Wozzeck seizes on his words: [*Vocal score: Act I, p. 61, bars 525 (with upbeat) – 531 (first half)*]. When finally, in the last variation, the Doctor breaks into a call for immortality – the most elevated of his obsessions – the bass theme which has been concealed in the course of the Passacaglia returns with renewed clarity, with chorale-like harmonies, and, in a kind of stretto, closes the movement [*Vocal score: Act I, p. 72, bars 638–55*]. As soon as this ends, the opening bars of the *Andante affettuoso* introduce the last scene of the first act.

The second act starts with the little orchestral introduction that you already know and has, as its first musical form, a sonata movement. It is not, perhaps, an accident that the three figures appearing in this scene, Marie, her child and Wozzeck, form the basis of the three thematic groups of the musical exposition – the first subject, second subject and coda – of a strict sonata structure. Indeed the whole of the dramatic development of this jewel scene, the twofold repetitions of certain situations and the confrontation of the main characters, lends itself to a strict musical articulation with an exposition, a first reprise, development and finally a recapitulation.

The following diagram makes this clear:

First subject: *Vocal score: Act II, p. 83, bars 7 (with upbeat) – 14*
Transition: *Vocal score: Act II, p. 84, bars 29–36*
Second subject: *Vocal score: Act II, p. 85, bars 43–6*
Coda: *Vocal score: Act II, p. 86, bars 55–9*
and with it ends the exposition.

The first reprise clearly repeats the exposition, although in a varied and shortened form. The development, that part of the scene in which the main figures (both human and musical) come into conflict, leads to the climax of the sonata, a statement of the leitmotive which runs through the whole work: [*Vocal score: Act I, p. 22, bar 136*; 'Wir arme Leut' – see Ex. 3, p. 27] Wozzeck's words 'Here is the money, Marie. My wages from the Captain and the Doctor' are sung to a held C major triad. How this C major triad (could the objectivity of money and what it represents be expressed more clearly!) leads to the final sonata recapitulation and thereby ends the Sonata, is shown by the remaining music of this scene and the subsequent orchestral interlude which, musically, belongs to and closes this scene.

That this orchestral interlude has an independent life of its own, and thus forms a separate musical unit, while, at the same time forming a link to what follows, can perhaps be demonstrated by the fact that the moment at which it begins is marked by a harp glissando, an effect which returns at the moment when the same interlude ends – the first of these a descending *ff* glissando, the second ascending *pp*. Please notice this as the orchestra now plays the recapitulation of this sonata as it grows out of the C major triad [*Vocal score: Act II, pp. 93–6, bars 123–70*].

The next scene also brings three people onto the stage, although, to be sure, their relationship to one another is looser than that of the three members of the family group in the previous scene. Whereas that scene could generate a musical structure (the sonata form) in which the parts were organically related, here the form is constructed from elements that stand in opposition to one another, that is to say, a fantasia and fugue on three themes. The motivic independence of these three themes, in contrast to the more closely related melodies of the previous sonata, itself suggests a strict fugal form, although the austerity of the form is, admittedly, somewhat relieved by the fact that it employs motives that have already been heard. That of the Captain has dominated his first scene at the very beginning of the opera: [*Vocal score: Act II, p. 97, bars 171–2 (Right hand)*]; that of the Doctor has appeared in the third scene of Act I: [*Vocal score: Act II, p. 97, bars 171–4 (Left hand)*]; while finally that of Wozzeck is a motive that has clearly been anticipated, even if it has not been literally stated, in the previous sonata movement: [*Vocal score: Act II, p. 108, bars 173–4*].

The slow movement of this symphonic act is a *Largo*. Apart from the obvious thematic relationships which make this *Largo* a self-contained movement it has one peculiarity: the instrumentation is that of chamber music and indeed corresponds exactly to the instrumentation of the *Chamber Symphony* of Arnold Schoenberg. I wanted here at the central point of the opera to pay homage to my teacher and master.

I want to take this opportunity to mention that in the instrumentation and orchestral layout of the whole opera I tried hard to take into account my desire to achieve, on the one hand, unity and integration and, on the other, variety and multiplicity. Not infrequently in this opera one finds sections or whole scenes, such as this, which are characterized by a specific instrumentation. Thus the sections of the little Suite in the first scene are each allotted a small instrumental obbligato group – five woodwind, or three drums and harp, or three flutes, or four brass instruments or a string quintet for example. One self-contained section of the second scene is wholly confined to the sound of muted brass and bowed *col legno* strings, a fugal section in the first scene of Act III to the sound of five solo strings. I should finally also mention the very last scene of the opera, the scene with the children, which does without the oboes, bassoons, trombones and double basses.

To return to the *Largo*. The way in which it is introduced and ended is also an example of the way in which a sense of self-containedness, of a kind that was formerly only possible by returning to the main key, can be achieved by other means. The clarinet figurations that emerge from the fugal material of the previous scene form a transition to this *Largo*, reaching an almost static chord [*Vocal score: Act II, p. 124, bars 365–6*] that acts as the harmonic foundation of the opening of the *Largo* theme: [*Vocal score: Act II,*

p. 124, bars 363–8]. The end of the *Largo* comes from the same harmony which, set in motion again, forms the retrograde of the same
clarinet figurations from which the chord originally developed:
[*Vocal score: Act II, p. 134, bars 406 (with upbeat) – 411*]. These clarinet figurations then lead into the subsequent orchestral interlude:
[*Vocal score: Act II, pp. 135–6*].

I would like to illustrate the symmetry of the architectural construction of this surrounding frame on the orchestra. The orchestra
will first play the introduction and the first of the *Largo* ideas and
will then play their musical mirror, the music that closes the scene
and leads into the interlude, which, in turn leads into the following
scene with a slow Ländler.

In this Ländler and in the other dance music you will find some
passages that might strike you as being 'dissonant' in a way that is
different from that of the strictly atonal music – dissonant in a way
similar to what might result if a number of pieces in different keys
were played at the same time, the sort of thing that you will have
heard at fairgrounds. This obvious dissonance springing from polytonality is intentional, of course, but it is not indiscriminate; it
springs not only from the dramatic situation but also from musical
logic. An example: the antecedent phrase of a Ländler in G minor
can, according to the rules of form, lead either to the dominant
(D major) or back to the tonic. It is the fact that both happen
together here (and who could blame a drunken pub-band for it!) that
causes the confusion here: [*Vocal score: Act II, p. 136, bars 424–5*].
Since one part of the band that has modulated to the dominant now
returns, according to the rules, to the tonic, G minor, while, at the
same time, the other, equally correctly, modulates to the relative
major, the confusion continues. It is a miracle that they all find
themselves back together again at the end of the Ländler.

Now I would like you to listen to this. As I've said, the orchestra
will first play the introduction to the *Largo*: [*Vocal score: Act II,
p. 123, bars 360 (with upbeat) – 372*] and then the retrograde passage
at the end which leads into the Ländler: [*Vocal score: Act II, p. 134,
bars 402 (with big upbeat) – 442*].

I have already said that the scene that now follows acts as the
scherzo of the dramatic symphony of this second act. The Ländler
which you have just heard is the first scherzo. A song by a travelling
apprentice represents the first trio, a waltz on the tavern band the
second scherzo and the hunting song of the young lads, the central
section of the whole thing, the second trio. There then follows, in

accordance with the strict structure of such scherzo movements (think, for example, of those in Schumann's symphonies), the reprise of the first three-part scherzo group. To be sure the reprise of these three little forms (Ländler, song and waltz) is not literal but is greatly varied, following the development of the dramatic action. Thus the Ländler, although repeated exactly, is placed in a quite new musical context. The first trio, represented by the song of the travelling apprentice, is repeated in so changed a manner that the harmonies on which it is based are split up to produce a chorale melody in semi-breves which, played by the bombardon, becomes the basis of the Melodrama. This melodrama, a harmless parody of a church sermon, is thus, on the one hand, the reprise of the first trio and, on the other hand, a strict (albeit a five-voice parody) chorale variation.

The repeat of the waltz of the tavern band does indeed finally appear as a waltz but, since it is at the same time the music of the interlude that leads to the next scene, it takes the more extensive form of a symphonic development section played on the full orchestra.

When this music is cut off we hear, at first from behind the closed curtain, the nature sound of the snoring chorus of soldiers in the barracks that I have already mentioned.

I have already spoken about the separate forms of Act III and the generating principles on which they are based. Scene 1 is based on the principle of a theme that is varied. The strictness of the architecture (I use the word intentionally) shows itself in that the two-part theme (antecedent and consequent) has seven bars, that there are seven variations, and the subject of the double fugue (reflecting the two parts of the theme) consists of seven notes.

It would be easy to make fun of the mathematical aspects of this form. As a matter of fact, that is what happened on the occasions of the first (concert) performance of this music, when a critic talked about the performance of this Bible scene, a performance that had not in reality even taken place. Although not a note of this music had been played, the keen-eared critic could confirm and could already tell his readers how bad such a mathematical organization would prove and how absurd it was that such things should exist.

The low B in the double basses that sounds with the final chord of this fugue (we already know it as the last note of the important closing cadence of Act II) now becomes the unifying force, the cohesive principle of the succeeding murder scene, although it also is, of course, treated in the most diverse ways imaginable – as a pedal point, as a fixed middle or upper voice, doubled in one or more octaves and appearing in all conceivable registers and timbres.

When the murder of Marie finally takes place to drum beats which gradually build up to *fortissimo*, all the important musical figurations associated with her are played very rapidly over this pedal point, as at the moment of her death the most important images of her life pass through her mind distorted and at lightning speed – the lullaby to her child from her first scene [*Vocal score: Act III, p. 196, bar 104*], reminiscences of the jewel scene [bar 104], the Drum Major himself [the same bar], the motive of Marie's sorrow over her misfortune [bar 105] and, finally, when she draws her last breath, the fifth motive of her hopeless waiting [bars 106–7] that I have already mentioned.

The music of the following short interlude brings the B♮ to the fore once more. This time it appears as a unison, as the only note of the entire scale common to almost all the instruments of a full orchestra, and beginning with the softest imaginable sound (a muted horn) and increasing through successively louder entries until it finally bursts out in full force on the whole orchestra, except percussion. A point to notice about these entries is that they are not at regular distances but follow a particular rhythmic principle in which the rhythmically ordered entries of the wind and strings, following one another in canon at the distance of a crotchet, produce a distinct rhythm. The irregularities that result from this – and of which the listener is as little aware as he is of the regular ordering of entries – seem to give the crescendoing note a particularly strong feeling of life. In fact this crescendo is of greater dynamic effect and intensity than the repetition of this crescendo on B in different registers and supported by the whole percussion group.

The rhythm that I have just mentioned is not, of course, accidental any more than is the chord to which the first of these crescendos leads: [*Vocal score, p. 197, chord, bar 114*] and which also has important thematic significance. The rhythm is that which forms the basis, and which, since it can be traced in every bar, guarantees the unity of the following scene. This rhythm is not, to be sure, superimposed upon the scene as an ever-present monotonous ostinato but is handled in such a way that it makes possible the greatest diversity, even metric diversity, within this quasi-rhythmic uniformity – as, for example, in the fast polka for the drunken lads and girls with which the scene begins: [*Vocal score: Act III, p. 198, bars 122–9*], or the following passage in which the rhythm becomes the accompaniment: [*Vocal score: Act III, p. 199, bars 145–52*], or those passages in which the rhythm is augmented, diminished or becomes displaced, as for example: [*Vocal score: Act III, p. 200, bars 152–9*], or in which the rhythm is accommodated in other metres, is divided into triplets or is presented as two or more overlapping canonic entries.

A similar example of a musical 'object' being used in this way, such as proved successful earlier when the object was a note or, as now, a rhythm (you will notice that this 'objectivity' is older than its present use as a catchword), can also be found in the following scene, which is entirely based on a chord or, to put it better, on a collection of six notes.

This chord has, as I said, already appeared in the earlier short interlude based on the big crescendo on B♮. It is also the harmonic complement to the end of the interlude of the previous scene: [*Vocal score, p. 210, bars 219–22*].

In spite of its being limited to this six-note collection, the scene again attempts to achieve both diversity and unity by subjecting the six-note chord, as had earlier been the case with the single note and the rhythm, to every possible kind of variation such as partitioning, inversion, redistribution and registral changes of the notes, for example: [*Vocal score, p. 213, bar 247, Vocal score, p. 217, bar 276*], and even dismantling the chord so that the notes are reinterpreted as melodies: [*Vocal score, p. 217, bars 278–83*].

Here again the overall structure of the piece is obtained through the use of the traditional symmetry of a ternary form, in that the six-note collection appears at only one transpositional level in the outer parts of the scene (although, obviously, in all varied forms) while in the central section it is transposed to all the other levels of the chromatic scale. When in the third part the chord returns to its original transpositional level – one might almost say that it goes back to its original tonal centre – it acts as the harmonic link to following interlude, the D minor of which represents the resolution of this six-note collection: [*Vocal score: Act III, pp. 223–4 with upbeat to D minor*]. More of this later. Just one general observation at the moment. It is clear that a music such as this, based solely on harmonies and superimposed chords, must, despite all its melodic features, have a strongly impressionistic character. That is, of course, something that is fitting for those dramatic events that are totally concerned with nature and natural phenomena. The waves in the pool as they close over the drowning Wozzeck or the croaking of the toads, for example: [*Vocal score: Act III, p. 222, bars 302–5*], or the rising of the moon: [*Vocal score: Act III, p. 222, bar 306*].

In spite of this, however, there was never any attempt at creating here a music of the kind one associates with Debussy and the French composers. Impressionism (to use yet another catchword of the last decades) of a kind that one might feel able to detect here and elsewhere in my opera can already be found in the music of the classical and romantic composers, to say nothing of the imperishable nature-impressionism of Wagner. In fact everything here that could be called impressionistic in this sense is far removed from the vague self-sufficient sonorities of that style; rather it has, as I have explained to you, much more to do with the building of a whole musical structure according to rigorous principles – provided here by the six-note chord, or in the second scene of Act I, about which we spoke earlier, by the repeated sequence of three chords.

The last scene of this act and of the whole opera, the scene with the children with its constant quaver movement from the first to the last bar (I could, referring back to older formal types, justifiably call it a 'perpetuum mobile'), is also governed by one ruling principle, although to be sure a principle that, as in other cases, I have laid down and required myself to follow.

The final scene, which you have heard, is preceded by a somewhat longer orchestral interlude. From the dramatic standpoint this interlude is to be understood as an 'Epilogue' following Wozzeck's suicide, as a confession of the author who now steps outside the dramatic action on the stage. Indeed, it is, as it were, an appeal to humanity through its representatives, the audience. From a musical standpoint this final orchestral interlude represents a thematic development of all the important musical ideas related to Wozzeck. It is a three-part structure and its organizing principle is, exceptionally, tonality. To be sure the frontiers of this D minor, the function of which as a harmonic resolution I have already mentioned, are so stretched as to reach the very limits of its influence, as indeed happens in the climactic middle section of this piece, where the tight compression of the entries results in an aggregate which contains all twelve notes, although in the context of this tonality it only acts as a dominant which leads naturally and convincingly back to the D minor of the reprise.

I should like to take this opportunity of thanking, with all my heart, the orchestra, its conductor Herr Musikdirector Johannes Schüler and the singers for their help. I shall now ask the orchestra to be kind enough to end my lecture by playing this epilogue, but I would first like to ask a favour of you – that you forget everything that I've tried to explain about musical theory and aesthetics when you come on Tuesday, or later, to see a performance of *Wozzeck* on the stage of this theatre.

First published in German in Hans Redlich, *Alban Berg: Versuch einer Würdigung*, Universal Edition, Vienna 1957, pp. 311–27

Notes

Introduction

1 For reasons that are explained in the following chapter the Büchner play is now known as *Woyzeck* and the Berg opera as *Wozzeck*.
2 'Firsthand reminiscence of a historic night', *San Francisco Chronicle*, 27 October 1981, p. 40
3 Wilhelm Worringer, *Formprobleme der Gothik*, Piper, Munich 1912. Quoted in Herbert Read, *A Concise History of Modern Painting*, Thames and Hudson, London 1959, p. 52
4 Read, *Concise History*, pp. 53ff
5 Alban Berg, *Letters to His Wife*, trans. Bernard Grun, Faber and Faber, London 1971, pp. 367f

2 The play and the libretto

1 Richard Hulsenbeck, *Die Dadaistische Bewegung. Eine Selbstbiographie*. Quoted in P. Raabe, *The Era of German Expressionism*, Calder and Boyars, London 1974, p. 352
2 Erwin Piscator, 'The proletarian theatre: its fundamental principles and task' (1920), reprinted in translation in Roger Howrad (editor), *Culture and Agitation*, Action Books, London 1972, p. 42
3 Arnold Schoenberg, 'The future of opera,' in *Style and Idea*, Faber and Faber, London 1975, p. 336
4 Quoted in Kim Kowalke, *Kurt Weill in Europe*, University of Michigan Press, Ann Arbor 1979, p. 3.
5 Quoted in Hans Moldenhauer, *Anton von Webern,* Gollancz, London 1978, p. 537
6 T. W. Adorno, *Alban Berg: der Meister des kleinsten Übergangs*, Elisabeth Lafite Verlag, Vienna 1968, p. 18

3 Musical background and composition

1 Willi Reich, *Arnold Schoenberg: A Critical Biography*, Longman, London 1971, p. 31
2 Mark DeVoto lists 'the 31 different themes' of the *Marsch* in 'Alban Berg's "Marche macabre"', *Perspectives of New Music*, 22/1 & 2, (Fall–Winter 1983 and Spring–Summer 1984).
3 Alban Berg, 'Open letter on the Chamber Concerto' in Willi Reich, *Alban Berg*, Thames and Hudson, London 1965, p. 145

4 Alban Berg, 'A word about *Wozzeck*'; see p. 153.
5 Douglas Jarman, *The Music of Alban Berg*, Faber and Faber, London 1979, p. 4
6 Alban Berg, *Briefe an seine Frau*, Langen Müller Verlag, Munich 1965, p. 507
7 Berg to Webern, 17 June 1924, quoted in Reich, *Berg*, p. 57
8 Ernst Hilmar, *Wozzeck von Alban Berg*, Universal Edition, Vienna 1975, p. 44
9 Reich, *Alban Berg*, p. 58
10 Alban Berg, *Letters to His Wife*, Faber and Faber, London 1971, p. 353
11 This account of the 'Schillings affair' is based on that given by Peter Heyworth in *Otto Klemperer: His Life and Times*, vol. 1, Cambridge University Press, Cambridge 1983, pp. 234ff.

5 The formal design

1 George Perle, 'Three views of *Wozzeck*', *Saturday Review*, 2 December 1967, p. 54
2 *Ibid.*, p. 55
3 *Ibid.*

7 A suggested interpretation

1 Victor Price, *The Plays of George Büchner*, Oxford University Press, London 1972, p. xvi
2 T. W. Adorno, *Berg, Der Meister des kleinsten Übergangs*, Elisabeth Lafite Verlag, Vienna 1968, p. 21
3 George Perle, *Serial Composition and Atonality*, 3rd edition, University of California Press, Berkeley 1972, p. 76
4 *Ibid.*
5 See George Perle, 'The secret program of the Lyric Suite', *Newsletter of the International Alban Berg Society*, 5 (June 1977), pp. 4ff
6 Alban Berg, *Letters to his Wife*, Faber and Faber, London 1971, p. 299
7 Kurt Blaukopf, 'New light on "Wozzeck"', *Saturday Review*, 26 September 1953, p. 62
8 *Ibid.*
9 See Erich Alban Berg, 'Eine natürliche Tochter. Zur Biographie Alban Berg', *Frankfurter Allgemeine Zeitung*, 21 May 1979, and 'Bergiana', *Schweizerische Musikzeitung*, 3 (May/June 1980), pp. 147–9.
10 Quoted in Douglas Jarman, 'Alban Berg. Wilhelm Fliess and the secret programme of the Violin Concerto', *Musical Times*, cxxiv, 1983, p. 218
11 Wilhelm Fliess, *Vom Leben und vom Tod*, Diedrich, Vienna 1909, p. 1
12 Berg, *Letters to His Wife*, pp. 112–13

8 Stage history: the premiere and subsequent performances

1 Reproduced in Konrad Vogelsang, *Dokumentation zur Oper 'Wozzeck' von Alban Berg*, Laaber Verlag, Regensburg 1977, p. 24
2 *Ibid.*

3 *Ibid.*, p. 20
4 *Ibid.*, p. 25
5 *Ibid.*, p. 22
6 *Ibid.*, p. 20
7 *Ibid.*, p. 21
8 *Ibid.*, p. 26
9 John Russell, *Erich Kleiber*, André Deutsch, London 1957, p. 121
10 Vogelsang, *Dokumentation*, p. 36
11 *Ibid.*, p. 34. On the Leningrad production of *Wozzeck* see Perle, *The Operas of Alban Berg*, vol. 1: *Wozzeck*, University of California Press, Berkeley 1980, pp. 199ff.
12 See p. 154.
13 Vogelsang, *Dokumentation*, p. 37
14 *Ibid.*, p. 39
15 *Ibid.*, p. 38
16 *Ibid.*, p. 37
17 Ernst Hilmar, *Wozzeck von Alban Berg*, Universal Edition, Vienna 1975, p. 44
18 *Ibid.*, p. 61
19 Vogelsang, *Dokumentation*, p. 64
20 *Ibid.*, p. 59
21 Hilmar, *Wozzeck*, p. 60
22 Volker Scherliess, *Alban Berg*, Rowohlt Taschenbuch, Hamburg 1975, p. 123
23 Hilmar, *Wozzeck*, p. 60
24 Vogelsang, *Dokumentation*, p. 44
25 *Ibid.*, p. 46
26 Walter Pass, 'Fur und Wider im Streit um die Wiener Erstaufführung des "Wozzeck"', in Otto Kolleritsch (editor), *50 Jahre Wozzeck von Alban Berg*, Universal Edition, Vienna 1978, p. 100
27 *Ibid.*, p. 100
28 Hans Moldenhauer, *Anton von Webern*, Gollancz, London 1978, p. 346
29 Hilmar, *Wozzeck*, p. 63
30 Pass, 'Für und Wider', p. 109
31 *Ibid.*, p. 101
32 Vogelsang, *Dokumentation*, p. 79
33 Alban Berg, *Letters to His Wife*, Faber and Faber, London 1971, p. 386
34 *Ibid.*, p. 384
35 Vogelsang, *Dokumentation*, p. 105
36 *Ibid.*, p. 48
37 Nicholas Slonimsky, *Music since 1900*, Cassell and Co., 4th edition, London 1972, p. 596
38 Nicholas Chadwick, 'Alban Berg and the BBC', *British Library Journal*, 2/1 (Spring 1985), p. 50
39 Hilmar, *Wozzeck*, p. 69
40 Chadwick, 'Berg and the BBC', p. 55
41 *Opera*, April 1950, p. 12
42 *Musical Times*, March 1952, p. 127
43 *Ibid.*, p. 1126

44 *New Statesman*, 43 (26 January 1952), p. 96
45 *Ibid.*, p. 96
46 *Sunday Times*, 27 January 1952
47 *Musical Times*, March 1952, p. 127
48 *Opera*, February 1952, p. 182
49 *Musical Times*, March 1952, p. 126
50 *Spectator*, 188 (1 February 1952), p. 141
51 *Musical Times*, March 1952, p. 116
52 *Opera*, May 1952, p. 411
53 *Musical America*, 15 April 1952, p. 5
54 *Opera*, February 1956, p. 99
55 Programme booklet, Deutsche Staatsoper Berlin, 1955
56 *Opera*, April 1959, p. 300
57 *Musical America*, March 1959, p. 3
58 *Saturday Review*, 21 March 1959, p. 32
59 *Time*, 73/11 (16 March 1959), p. 52
60 Perle, *The Operas*, vol. 1, p. 205
61 Pierre Boulez, '"Wozzeck" and its interpretation', in J. J. Nattiez (editor), *Orientations*, trans. Martin Cooper, Faber and Faber, London 1986, p. 378
62 George Perle, 'Three views of "Wozzeck"', *Saturday Review*, 2 December 1967, p. 54
63 *Ibid.*

Bibliography

The bibliography includes details of all the books mentioned in the preceding text and a selection of the most important of other relevant writings. A full list of the articles and books on the Büchner play and the Berg opera would run to many hundreds of entries; the following bibliography makes no attempt to be comprehensive.

Adorno, T.W., *Alban Berg: der Meister des kleinsten Übergangs*, Elisabeth Lafite Verlag, Vienna 1968

Berg, Alban, *Letters to His Wife*, Faber and Faber, London 1971

Berg, Erich Alban, 'Bergiana', *Schweizerische Musikzeitung*, 3, May/June 1980, pp. 147–9

'Eine natürliche Tochter: zur Biographie Alban Berg', *Frankfurter Allgemeine Zeitung*, 21 May 1975

Blaukopf, Kurt, 'New light on "Wozzeck"', *Saturday Review*, 26 September 1953

DeVoto, Mark, 'Alban Berg's "Marche macabre"', *Perspectives of New Music*, 22/1 & 2, Fall–Winter 1983 and Spring–Summer 1984

Elbogen, Paul, 'Firsthand reminiscence of a historic night', *San Francisco Chronicle*, 27 October 1981, p. 40

Heyworth, Peter, *Otto Klemperer: His Life and Times*, vol. 1, Cambridge University Press, Cambridge 1983

Hilmar, Ernst, *Wozzeck von Alban Berg: Entstehung, erste Erfolg, Repression*, Universal Edition, Vienna 1975

Hilmar, Rosemary, *Alban Berg, Leben und Wirken in Wien bis zur seinen ersten Erfolgen als Komponist*, Verlag Hermann Bohlaus Nachf., Vienna 1978

Howrad, Roger (ed.), *Culture and Agitation*, Action Books, London 1972

Jarman, Douglas, *The Music of Alban Berg*, Faber and Faber, London 1979

Jouve, Pierre Jean, and Fano, Michel, *Wozzeck d'Alban Berg*, Edition Plon, Paris 1953

Kolleritsch, Otto (ed.), *50 Jahre Wozzeck*, Universal Edition, Vienna 1975

König, Werner, *Tonalitätstrukturen in Alban Bergs Oper 'Wozzeck'*, Hans Schneider, Tutzing 1974

Kowalke, Kim, *Kurt Weill in Europe*, University of Michigan Press, Ann Arbor, 1979

Moldenhauer, Hans, *Anton von Webern*, Gollancz, London 1978

Perle, George, *The Operas of Alban Berg*, vol. 1: *Wozzeck*, University of California Press, Berkeley, 1980

'The secret program of the Lyric Suite', *Newsletter of the International Alban Berg Society*, 5, June 1977

Serial Composition and Atonality, 3rd edition, University of California Press, Berkeley, 1972

'Three views of "Wozzeck"', *Saturday Review*, 2 December 1967, pp. 54ff

Ploebsch, Gerd, *Alban Bergs 'Wozzeck': Dramaturgie und musikalische Aufbau*, Sammlung Musikwissenschaftlicher Abhandlungen, vol. 48, Verlag Heitz, Strasbourg 1968

Price, Victor, *The Plays of Georg Büchner*, Oxford University Press, London 1972

Raabe, Paul, *The Era of German Expressionism*, Calder and Boyars, London 1974

Read, Herbert, *A Concise History of Modern Painting*, Thames and Hudson, London 1959

Redlich, Hans, *Alban Berg, the Man and his Music*, John Calder, London 1957

Reich, Willi, *Alban Berg*, Thames and Hudson, London 1965

Arnold Schoenberg, A Critical Biography, Longman, London 1971

Russell, John, *Erich Kleiber*, André Deutsch, London 1957

Scherliess, Volker, *Alban Berg*, Rowohlt Taschenbuch, Hamburg 1975

Schmalfeldt, Janet, *Berg's 'Wozzeck': Harmonic Language and Design*, Yale University Press, New Haven 1983

Schoenberg, Arnold, *Style and Idea*, Faber and Faber, London 1975

Vogelsang, Konrad, *Dokumentation zur Oper 'Wozzeck' von Alban Berg*, Laaber Verlag, Regensburg 1977

Discography

All recordings are stereo.

Deutsche Grammophon: DGG 2707/023

Conductor: Karl Böhm
Cast: Dietrich Fischer-Dieskau (Wozzeck), Evelyn Lear (Marie), Helmut Melchert (Drum Major), Fritz Wunderlich (Captain), Gerhard Stolze (Andres), Karl Christian Kohn (Doctor), Alice Oelke, (Margret), Kurt Böhme, Robert Koffmane, Martin Vantin, Walter Muggelberg
Berlin State Opera Orchestra and Chorus
Recording released 1965; reissued (DG 413 804–1) 1985

CBS: SET 3003

Conductor: Pierre Boulez
Cast: Walter Berry (Wozzeck), Isabel Strauss (Marie), Fritz Uhl (Drum Major), Albert Weikenmeier (Captain), Richard van Vrooman (Andres), Carl Doench (Doctor), Ingeborg Lasser (Margret), Walter Poduschka, Raymond Steffner, Gerard Dunan
Paris National Opera Orchestra and Chorus
Recording released 1965; reissued (CBS 79251) 1971

Decca: D231 D2

Conductor: Christoph von Dohnanyi
Cast: Eberhard Waechter (Wozzeck), Anja Silja (Marie), Hermann Winkler (Drum Major), Heinz Zednik (Captain), Horst Laubenthal (Andres), Alexander Malta (Doctor), Gertrude Jahn (Margret), Alfred Sramek, Franz Waechter, Walter Wendig, Michael Pabst
Vienna Philharmonic Orchestra and Vienna State Opera Chorus
Recording released 1981

Index

(Italicized page numbers refer to pages in the central photographic section of the book. References to newspaper, periodical or other bibliographic material are excluded. Musical compositions and literary works appear under the name of the composer or author when that name appears in the text.)

Abendroth, Martin, 69
Adorno, Theodor Wiesengrund, 10, 62–3
Aida (Verdi), 144
Amis, John, 83
Anderson, W. R., 84
Aravantinos, Panos, 69, *92*
Austin, Sumner, 82

Bachrich, Ernst, 24
Bartered Bride, The (Smetana), 72
Bartosch, Konrad, 74
Baudelaire, Charles
  Une Charogne, 83
Beiber, Hugo, 5, 110
  'Wozzeck and Woyzeck' 129–32
Berg, Alban
  autobiographical elements in music of, 68ff
  compositions: *Altenberg Lieder*, Op. 4, 5, 18, 19, 20, 21; *Drei Bruchstücke aus 'Wozzeck'*, 23; Four Pieces for Clarinet and Piano, Op. 5, 19, 21, 132; *Lulu*, 2, 18, 43, 63, 86, 89; *Lyric Suite*, 79, 110; Piano Sonata, Op. 1, 18, 132; Piano Sonata No. 4 (early), *91*; Schliesse mir die Augen beide, 20, 110; String Quartet Op. 3, 5, 17, 23, 132, 133; *Symphonic Pieces from 'Lulu'*, 79; *Three Orchestral Pieces*, Op. 6, 5, 19, 20, 21, 22, 23, 88, 89, 132; *Vier Lieder*, Op. 2, 17, 20; Violin Concerto, 20–1, 63; see also *Wozzeck*
  musical development of, 17–20

musical language, characteristics of, 20–1
  numerological interests, 63, 67
  writings: 'A lecture on "Wozzeck"', 59, 111, 154–70; 'The musical forms in my opera "Wozzeck"', 111, 149–52; 'The Musical Impotence of Hans Pfitzner', 111; 'The preparation and staging of "Wozzeck"', 84, 88, 89; 'A word about "Wozzeck"', 6, 41, 89, 111, 152–4
Berg, Helene, 5, 66, 67, 78
Bie, Oskar, 69
Bing, Rudolf, 87
Bitterauf, Richard, 80, *94, 95, 96, 97*
Böhm, Karl, 81, 86
Boris Godunov (Mussorgsky), 78
Boulez, Pierre, 88, 89
Boult, Adrian, 80
Brecht, Bertolt, 10, 11, 74
Britten, Benjamin
  Peter Grimes, 3
Brücke, Die, 3
Brugmann, Walter, *106*
Bruhn, Alice, *94, 95, 97*
Büchner, Alexander, 115, 118, 119
Büchner, Georg, 1, 3, 5, 16, 24, 60, 76, 77, 84, 86, 110, 111–32, 148, 151, 152, 154
  biography, 7–8
  works: *Dantons Tod*, 7, 9, 11, 125, 126; *Der hessische Landbot*, 7, 118; *Lenz*, 7, 112; *Leonce und Lena*, 8, 9, 128; *Pietro Aretino*, 8, 125; *Woyzeck* (see under *W*.)
Büchner, Ludwig, 112–32
  Kraft und Stoff, 112, 126

Büchner, Luise, 115, 118, 119
Bukofzer, Manfred, 74
Busoni, Ferruccio, 2

Carmen (Bizet), 143
Clark, Edward, 80
Clarus, J. C. A., 8, 130
Cooper, Martin, 83

Dalberg, Fredrick, 82
Dallapiccola, Luigi, 10
Dean, Winton, 83
Dessau, Paul, 86
Dobujinsky, Mstislav, 84, 85
Dranschikov, Vladimir, 72
Drath, Johannes, *104, 105*

Eisler, Hanns, 86
Elbogen, Paul, 1
Engels, Friedrich, 86
Erhardt, Otto, 80
Etienne, Michael, 112, 113, 121
Eugene Onegin (Tchaikovsky), 143
Eulenberg, Herbert, 129
Expressionism, 3, 9, 10
Eyre, Ronald, 87

Fauves, Les, 3
Fidelio (Beethoven), 71, 83, 84, 143
Fliess, Wilhelm, 67
Franzos, Karl Emil, 5, 8, 110, 140
  '*Georg Büchner*', 111–29
Friedrichs, Emma, *93*
Fuchs-Robettin, Hanna, 63
Furtwängler, Wilhelm, 79

Garten, Hugo, 81
Gebrauchsmusik, 10
Glebov, Igor, 72
Gluck, Christoph Willibald von, 2, 149
Gobbi, Tito, 81
Goebbels, Joseph, 79
Goethe, Johann Wolfgang von, 112,
  119, 126, 131
Gogol, Nikolai, 112
Goltz, Christel, 82
Grabbe, Christian Dietrich, 126, 149
Graf, Herbert, 87
Grillparzer, Franz, 116
Groening-Altona, Karl, *109*
Guzkow, Karl, 117

Hagner, Walter, *105*
Hannesson, Thorenstein, 82

Hans Heiling (Marschner), 145, 150
Hauptmann, Gerhart, 129
Havemann Quartet, 23
Hebbel, Friedrich, 149
Heine, Heinrich, 112
Heinsheimer, Hans, 73
Henke, Adolf, 131
Henke, Waldemar, 69
Hertzka, Emil, 22
Hill, Hainer, 85
Hindemith, Paul, 79
Horenstein, Jascha, 19
Hörth, Franz Ludwig, 69
Humboldt, Alexander von, 117

Jacobs, Arthur, 81
Jaegle, Minna, 8, 114
Jalowetz, Heinrich, 75, 80
Jenůfa (Janáček), 84
Jessner, Leopold, 9
Johanson, Sigrid, 69
Jones, Parry, 82
Jones, Robert Edmund, 102
Jürgens, Helmut, *94*

Kassowitz, Gottfried, 11, 66
Kelch, Werner, 85
Kleiber, Erich, 24, 69, 72, 79, 82, 85, 87
Klein, Fritz Heinrich, 6, 22, 110, 111,
  139
  'Alban Berg's "Wozzeck"', 135–8
Kleist, Heinrich von, 149
Kolodin, Irving, 87
Komisarjevsky, Theodore, 84, 85
Korngold, Julius, 77
Krasner, Louis, 78
Krauss, Otokar, 82

Landau, Paul, 9, 146
Lenz, Jakob Michael Reinhold, 112
Lex, Josef, 74, *93*
Liebstockl, Hans, 77
Lohman, Albert, *98*, 101
Lortzing, Gustav Albert, 149
Ludwig, Anton, *96*

Mahler, Fritz, 41
Mahler, Gustav, 19, 20, 71
Mann, William, 82, 83
Markwort, Peter, *104, 105*
Matisse, Henri, 3
Meyer, Hans, 86
Meyer, Richard M., 140
Minten, Reiner, *106, 107*

Mitropolous, Dimitri, 81
Mittrovic, Anita, *99*
Monteverdi, Claudio, 2, 71
Mozart, Wolfgang Amadeus, 45, 139, 149
Munch, Edvard, 3

Neher, Caspar, 75, 76, 82, 87
Neoclassicism, 10
Neue Sachlichkeit, 10
Neumann, Karl August, *106, 107, 108*
Newman, Ernest, 83
Nolde, Emil, 3

Osterkamp, Ernst, *108*
Ostrčil, Otokar, *71, 72*

Paradiso (Dante), 84
Pella, Paul, *94*
Pelléas et Mélisande (Debussy), 77, 78
Perle, George, 50, 51, 59
Petschnig, Emil, 6, 23, 111, 149, 150, 151
'Creating atonal opera', 143–9
Pisling, Wiegmund, 70
Price, Victor, 80

Read, Herbert, 3, 4
Recka, Erna, *103*
Redlich, Hans, 111
Rehm, Kurt, 85
Reinhardt, Max, 9
Rosenthal, Harold, 81
Rosenstock, Joseph, 84
Rothmüller, Marko, 82, 84

Sabin, Robert, 84
Sale, Frank, 82
Sattler, Joachim, *101*
Sauerlaender, Remy, 124, 125, 127
Scherchen, Hermann, 23
Scheuchl, Albine, 67
Scheuchl, Marie, 67
Schiller, Johann Christoph Friedrich von
Die Räuber, 126
Schillings, Max von, 24
Schocke, Johannes, *98*
Schoenberg, Arnold, 6, 10, 16, 17, 19, 22, 23, 67, 69, 70, 71, 76, 77, 80, 86, 91, 110, 132, 135, 139, 154, 155
compositions: Chamber Symphony No. 1, 18, 22, 133, 164; *Erwartung*, 16, 71, 139, 140; Five Orchestral

Pieces, Op. 16, 16, 139; *Die glückliche Hand*, 139, 160; *Pelleas und Melisande*, 18; *Pierrot lunaire*, 73, 140, 147, 154, 160; String Quartet No. 1, 16, 18; String Quartet No. 2, 17; *Verklärte Nacht*, 16
writings: *Harmonielehre*, 17
Schreker, Franz, 139–40
Der ferne Klang, 140
Schüler, Johannes, 73, 74, 85, 169
Schützendorf, Leo, 69
Seider, August, *108*
Serafin, Tullio, 81
Shakespeare, William, 126, 147
Shawe-Taylor, Desmond, 82
Sievert, Ludwig, *103*
Society for Private Musical Performances, *see* Verein für musikalische Privataufführungen
Soot, Fritz, 69
Stalin, Josef, 86
Steber, Eleanor, 86
Stefan, Paul, 70
Stein, Erwin, 6, 23, 81, 110
'Alban Berg and Anton Webern', 132–5
Steinrück, Albert, 1
Stern, Jan, *103*
Stokowski, Leopold, 77
Strauss, Richard, 140
Elektra, 71, 140
Der Rosenkavalier, 145, 150
Salome, 145, 150
Stravinsky, Igor, 19, 71
The Rite of Spring, 19
Strohm, Heinrich, *94*
Stuckenschmidt, H. H., 70

Thoran, Corneil de, 78
Tonality
as an organizational system, 16–17
breakdown of, 17
Trapp, Lothar Schenk von, *98*
Turgenev, Ivan Sergevich, 112

Uhde, Herman, 86
Universal Edition, 22, 23, 71, 73, 74, 76, 77

Van Gogh, Vincent, 3
Verein für musikalische Privataufführungen, 22
Viebig, Ernst, 6, 23, 111, 143, 144, 145, 149

'Alban Berg's "Wozzeck": a contribution to the problem of opera', 139–43
Vogt, Karl, 129

Wagner, Richard, 2, 18, 72, 146, 149
  Die Meistersinger, 143
  Tristan und Isolde, 71
Walters, Jess, 82
Weber, Carl Maria von, 146, 150
Webern, Anton, 6, 10, 17, 19, 23, 74, 77, 110, 132–5
Wedekind, Frank, 129
Weill, Kurt, 2, 10, 11, 75
  Der Aufstieg und Fall der Stadt Mahagonny, 11
  Die Dreigroschenoper, 10
Weissman, Adolf, 70, 71
Werner, T. W., 74
Wiedig, Friedrich Ludwig, 7
Wiene, Robert, 10
  The Cabinet of Dr Caligari, 10
Witting, Gerhard, 69
Witokowski, Georg, 140
Worringer, Wilhelm, 3
Worthley, Max, 82
Woyzeck (Büchner), 8, 16, 60
  background to, 8
  Berg's changes to, 11–12
  first performance of, 9
  preparation and publication of, 8–9, 110–29
  Viennese premiere of, 1
  expressionist elements in, 3
Woyzeck, Johann Christian, 8, 110, 129–32
Wozzeck (Berg)
  analysis of (Act III scene 4), 52–8
  autobiographical elements in, 66–8
  banning of, 72, 78–80ff
  composition of, 1, 21–4
  curtains in, 50–1, 61
  formal design of, 41–51, 60–1, 133, 135–70
  formal design, dramatic significance of, 43–4, 61, 65–8, 135–70

libretto of, 11–15
  motivic structure of, 45–9, 54–5
  performances of
    cancellations: Coburg, 78; Mainz, 78
    premieres: Aachen, 75, *94–97*; Berlin, 24, 69–71, *92*; Braunschweig, 77; Brussels, 78; Cologne, 75; Darmstadt, 77, *98–101*; Düsseldorf, 75; Essen, 75–6; Frankfurt, 77, *103*; Freiburg, 77; Gera, 75; Königsberg, 75; Leipzig, 77, *106–8*; Leningrad, 72–3; London (concert performance), 80; Lübeck, 75; Oldenburg, 73–4, *93*; Philadelphia, 77–8, *102*; Prague, 71–2; Rome, 80; Vienna, 76; Wuppertal, 77, *104–5*; Zurich, 77, *109*
    projected: Covent Garden, 80
    revivals: Berlin (1932), 79
    post-war productions: Berlin (1955), 85–6; Düsseldorf (1948), 81; Hamburg (1953), 85; Hannover (1955), 85; Heidelburg (1954), 85; Kassel (1955), 74; Kiel (1953), 85; London (1949, concert perf.), 81; London (1952), 81–4; Milan (1952), 85; Naples (1950), 81; New York (1951, concert perf.), 81; New York (1952, N.Y. City Opera), 84–5; New York (1959, Met.), 86–7; Oldenburg (1953), 85; Paris (1950), 81; Salzburg (1951), 81; Scottish Opera (1980), 89; Vienna (1952), 85; Vienna (1987), 90; Welsh Opera (1986), 90; Wiesbaden (1953), 85; Wuppertal (1954), 85
  plot of, 25–40
  Sprechstimme in, 88–9
  time, significance of, 61–5

Zimmermann, George, 117
Zschorlich, Paul, 69, 70